St Vincent
and The Grenadines

(2nd Edition)

Lesley Sutty

CARIBBEAN

For Michael M.

First published 1997 by
MACMILLAN EDUCATION LTD
London and Basingstoke
Companies and representatives throughout the world

ISBN 0–333–71353–2

10   9   8   7   6   5   4   3   2
06   05   04   03

This book is printed on paper suitable for recycling and
made from fully managed and sustained forest sources.

Printed in Malaysia

A catalogue record for this book is available from the
British Library.

Front cover: Michael Bourne
Back cover: Lesley Sutty

| Contents |

iii

Coastal profiles of the islands

Pigeon I

Petit Mustique (from 5.75 miles at 38°N)

Isle à Quatre

Mustique (from 7 miles)

Bequia

St Vincent

Baliceaux

Battowia

Petit Canouan (from 9 miles at 79°N)

Savan Rock

Isle Savan (from 5.5 miles)

Le Pic (from 7.25 miles at 26°N)

Canouan

Mayero (from 7.75 miles)

Catholic Island

Dove C. Colle. du Taffia

Union Island (from 10.75 miles)

C. de Sable

Tobago Cays (from 6 miles)

Frigate Island

Palm Island

Isle Rouge

Carriacou

Petite Martinique (from 9.5 miles)

Petit St. Vincent (from 9 miles)

iv

Introduction

Twenty-five million years ago an oceanic island spread from the north coast of Bequia to the southern Reindeer Shoals of Grenada. At the end of the tertiary era, and with the melting of the great ice masses, the sea inundated the low-lying valleys and plains to create an archipelago of more than eighty islands and islets, all of them later fringed with coral. This haven of marine life was ninety miles long and only three miles wide. The thin submarine strip known as the Grenada Bank was forty metres deep at its most, plunging deeply to six hundred metres on its northern extremity. Here nine miles of tumultuous seas separated the island of Bequia from its parent, St Vincent.

Many of the archipelagans never ventured outside their own territory whilst others travelled great distances on the sloops and top-masted schooners built by their own hands. These vessels transported provisions and water to the small dependencies in time of drought. Without a single water source life became cruel and often fatal for livestock and infants in arms. Carême, the dry season, was so unpredictable some years that it seemed eternal, and the scant rain clouds which were supposed to fill the waiting cisterns meanly shed their water on the surface of the sea, in the passes and channels dividing each land mass, little more than dampening the pure silky sands of the still lagoons.

Twenty-five years ago when I sailed this archipelago and explored its reefs and ocean there were as many large fish as there were small ones, all of them curious and friendly. The only other ships we saw were the trading schooners, and the beaches were deserted with only the royal terns keeping watch. Great iguanas lazed in the sun as the fishermen went quietly about their business. Pink conchs carpeted the seagrass beds, and turtles basked on the surface. Silver tarpons spun through the air to plunge into the great schools of jacks and anchovy, on which the pelicans and their young also feasted. Parrot and angel fish paid little heed to the passing dolphins, whales and orcas. Hammerhead and great white sharks roamed the deep offshore waters – and were sometimes ensnared in the fishermen's

1

nets. The shades of turquoise, jades and blues of the lagoons were endless.

The mother island, St Vincent, was majestic, with dense rainforest and rushing rivers. Countless coconut trees and palms shaded groves and sustained the land. Steep ledges plunged into the sea where the submarine realm and its cliffs were an explosion of life.

The Grenada Bank from the air (opposite) (LESLEY SUTTY)

Sailing yacht *La Constance* off St Vincent (LESLEY SUTTY)

Tellina from the Grenadines (LESLEY SUTTY)

How long could such perfection remain a secret? There was neither water nor electricity in the Grenadines. Twice a day the cows headed for the sea to quench their thirst. There was little means of cultivating a kitchen garden; it was a fight with the elements and errant cattle to raise a few heads of corn or a small field of pigeon peas and sweet potatoes, which might survive until Christmas. When the rains didn't come between New Year and Easter the land turned to dust, and became parched and cracked. Dried leather hides and bones replaced the sturdy herds of bovines. These were the bad years when even the ancient artesian wells went dry.

In the early 1970s this unique and magical chain of islands caught the eye of speculators, and within fifteen years another world had been created. The coral reef ecosystem suffered dangerously from this invasion, but the quality of so much beauty was impervious to human advance.

The people of St Vincent and the Grenadines are without doubt the proudest islanders I have encountered. They are a rare breed whose lives have often been governed by hardship, even when surrounded by nature's magnificence, and to whom I have become deeply attached.

Lesley Sutty

| 1 |
The first migrants – Ciboneys, Arawaks, Calivignies and Caribs

Archaeological research reveals that the prehistoric settlements of the Grenadine Islands are the last intact chronological evidence of the multiple cultures migrating from the South American mainland via the Guyana Highlands, and from regions as far apart as Colombia to Brazil, towards the northern river deltas and the Caribbean Sea. The great diversity of ceramic styles devised by these people has remained untouched and separated by the strata of many time eras, buried beneath dense growths of bush, scrub and alluvium.

Stone Age men first explored the islands some 7000 years ago. These hunter-gatherers were called Ciboneys; they ate wild fruits and berries and harvested the shallow water seashells and the pink conch. They left behind them, on cliffs and beside salt ponds, roughly-hewn stone and shell hand-tools and axes. They did not make pottery but used the shells of the calabash fruit as receptacles. These nomads were slowly assimilated by following cultures.

The Arawaks, who migrated to the islands at least two hundred years before Christ, travelled in fifty-foot dugouts, carrying with them fire-burners, animals and plants. Their landfalls were governed by the westerly currents, winds and storms. On clear days it was possible to see Grenada from the mountain summits of Venezuela. The various pottery styles that have been excavated indicate that for 2000 years Saladoids, Barrancoids, Huecoids, Guapoids, Arawaks, Galibis or Caribs successively arrived in the Grenadines and St Vincent. Cassava, corn and fruits were cultivated by these early settlers.

A period of peace known to no other civilisation in the history of mankind ruled over the West Indian island territories for 1500

A Carib *ajoupa* (LESLEY SUTTY)

Petroglyphs, St Vincent (LESLEY SUTTY)

years. The Arawaks were totally unprepared for invasion by the Caribs, who killed their men and carried off their women. At the same time a small group of Calivignoid Indians arrived in the archipelago. They made pottery with strange geometric designs and dolls with pronounced eyebrows and noses.

Each tribe in its turn discovered the wealth of the sea. They settled close to rivers or the streams that flowed in the wet seasons, facing the barrier reefs. On the islands were dense woods. The people dug deep wells to filter sea-water. They used the sap of the manchioneel tree to poison their arrows for the hunt. Some of these migrants were named 'crab cultures', as their kitchen middens were made up of great mounds of crab shells and claws. They lived in thatched huts made from palms and seagrape wood and, having become seasoned navigators, they journeyed throughout the islands exchanging stone, shell, sponge, cloth and pottery. They made beautiful amulets and necklaces which were carried as gifts for newly-weds, shamans or chiefs of neighbouring tribes.

The Arawak women who had been captured and enslaved by the Caribs refused to speak their masters' language and with time the ancient Tupi-Arawakan language died out together with the beautiful incised and painted ceramics which had been made by these female potters.

The Caribs were good and strong swimmers, quite unafraid of sharks and used to the large catfish of the fresh water deltas. Their art was not decorative but unusually figurative and appealing.

| 2 |
The era of discovery

Hairoun, Youroumei, meaning humans or *lucanas* in the Indian language, was a land blessed with rainbows, mist, fertile valleys and sun. Its verdant foliage fell luxuriantly from the cliffs; sparkling torrents and waterfalls freshened the forests. A great volcano rose 4000 feet above the land, a mysterious, strange place.

Christopher Columbus sighted the island on 22 January 1498 on his third voyage. He called the island St Vincent, after the Spanish saint St Vincent, whose feast day it was, as he sailed by in his caravel. Both fifteenth and sixteenth century chronicles imply that St Vincent had not been earmarked for immediate conquest, for the quest for gold took priority. Also a large native population was reported to inhabit the island, and had fiercely repelled the first attempted landings. Vessels from the east gave the island a wide berth and did not dare to breach the uncharted mass of coral reefs of the Grenadines, or Grenadinos (little Grenadas) as they were called by the Spanish. In 1595 Sir Walter Raleigh anchored briefly off St

La Soufrière, St Vincent's volcano (LESLEY SUTTY)

Vincent, carrying away with him an impression that the land was inhabited by cannibals and savages.

The first white settlers were two French missionaries, who are thought to have settled at Chateaubelair. Father Aubergeon had been invited to visit the island in 1653 by the Carib Indians, who wished to show their gratitude for the return of their young men, who had been abducted for questioning. Within a year this priest and his companion estimated that 10,000 Caribs lived on the island. Shortly after this census was taken a total lack of understanding was responsible for a serious confrontation between the proud Carib leaders and those who had come to convert and reform them. The small mission was burnt to the ground and its inhabitants massacred. News of this act quickly reached Martinique, and an expeditionary force of three men-o-war with troops was sent to St Vincent to carry out punitive action. Carib men, women and children were slaughtered, their villages and crops burned.

When the Caribs saw the first runaway negro slaves their astonishment must have been considerable. News had been carried to nearby islands that men were free on St Vincent. Angered by their recent punishment, they must have felt some sympathy for these freedom seekers, who had braved the ocean, often alone. By 1676 some 3000 negroes lived on St Vincent, making up more than a third of the population. The Caribs condoned this quest for freedom by runaway slaves, and no longer sold them back to their masters, when tales of the cruel and terrible punishments dealt to the escapees was carried back to the tribal chiefs.

This negro population was nearly all male, and the need for women was great. Skirmishes to carry off Indian women were increasingly frequent. The negroes of African origin and skills proved serious opponents, and the Caribs were obliged to seek a compromise. Born of Indian mothers and African fathers, the 'Black Caribs' were quickly to outnumber those who had welcomed them, the 'Yellow Caribs'.

| 3 |
The tale of
the Black Caribs

Resentment between the Black and Yellow Caribs increased daily and the situation was monitored with interest by the French, who wished to oust the British garrison and claim St Vincent for themselves. They also saw such a clash as a potential source of slaves and agreed to help the Yellow Caribs remove the Black Caribs from St Vincent. The Black Caribs had by now become skilful soldiers and were most often victorious during the several attacks carried out on their settlements at the beginning of the eighteenth century. They had been given weapons by French farmers who had tried to be conciliatory towards the Indians when first marking out their lands, and more so towards the leaders of the Black Caribs, provisioning them additionally with wines and cognac. This trading encouraged the Black Caribs to speak French, and participate in religious ceremonies. Many of them had French names, such as Jean-Baptiste, François and Duvalle. One of them, Chatoyer, became a flamboyant Black Carib chief, who frequently indulged in guerilla warfare.

Charles I had granted this British Dominion to the Earl of Carlisle in 1627. It was more than a hundred years later, when the island was the property of the Duke of Montagu, that the decision was taken to form a colony. The troops sent from England, burdened by their heavy uniforms and without any knowledge of the terrain, were quick to realise the need for different tactics.

The series of private land treaties made out between Caribs and French settlers were declared null and void. In 1762 the Treaty of Paris allocated territories to the British. St Vincent was part of the British concessions. Although many sympathised with the Caribs, in 1773 George II drew up a peace treaty for the island which William Dalrymple presented to the Carib chiefs for signature. The twenty-four French speaking chiefs understood little of the deep meaning of the articles of the treaty. Slowly but surely they were shifted to increasingly smaller reserves. The large Black Carib

11

Chatoyer, the chief of the Black Caribs (from an engraving of 1773, Agostina Brunyas)

community felt outraged and insulted and renewed hostilities in the hope of reclaiming their lands, if not their rights. They requested help from the Governor of Martinique. In 1779 a French vessel headed for St Vincent with five hundred fighting men on board. On landing they managed to stop the Caribs from massacring all the settlers and the British Governor. Governor Morris surrendered to Captains DuRumaine and Percin de la Roche, who had been backed by a strange army of free negroes, Black Caribs and mulattoes. In 1784 the island was restored to the British at a time when Martinique was also a Crown Colony. In 1796 Chatoyer and his general, Duvalle, headed the last of the Carib uprisings. This was to be one of considerable slaughter and plundering, with the destruction of many estates. The British took to arms, destroying most of the native crops and villages. This battle lasted ten days, and ended with a final duel between Major Leith and Chatoyer. Chatoyer was quickly struck down, and order was restored.

During his lifetime Chatoyer had been respected by all. His death left his people without a leader. Sir Ralph Abercrombie arrived in the Caribbean in 1796 accompanied by several thousand soldiers. The force landed on St Vincent and from this moment the Black Caribs had no further legal or moral rights. What remained of villages, crops and vessels was ruthlessly destroyed and reduced to ashes. The people fled to the furthest hiding places in the mountainous regions, but the hunger of the women and children was decisive.

Journey into exile

General Abercrombie, together with Sir William Young, decided as a final plan of action to ship the Caribs to Roatan and the Bay Islands of Honduras. They delivered an ultimatum to the Black Carib chiefs in July of 1796, leaving them little alternative. Only 280 of their numbers turned up for the planned shipping. Miserably they embarked on a vessel which would take them to a transit point on Baliceaux, an inhospitable island in the south. The remaining five thousand Caribs were hunted down to be transported to Roatan just one year after Chatoyer had led his people into final war. Their beautiful island Youroumei, land of the blessed and rainbows, disappeared in the mist and from their view for ever.

Epilogue

The Yellow Caribs, who had lived quietly on the northern point at Sandy Bay, had avoided the terrors of war and some two hundred Indians continued to live there in a small reserve, whilst the hardiest of the Black Caribs, a handful of men and women, had retreated far into the wooded areas of Greiggs.

Carib children (LESLEY SUTTY)

What became of those Black Caribs who were shipped to Honduras? Today, some two hundred years later, some 40,000 Black Caribs live in Central America, from Costa Rica to Yucatan and Honduras. Descendants of those who survived at Greiggs still live there.

In the old officers' quarters at Fort Charlotte there is an exhibition of paintings by Lindsay Prescott which recounts the history of the Black Caribs.

| 4 |
Of men, women and children

A British Colony from 1783 to 1969, when it became an Associated State, the island of St Vincent and its dependencies the Grenadines became fully independent on 27 October 1979. There is now a population of some 120,000 of which 60% are black, 23.5% metis, 5.5% white and 2% Amerindian. The state covers an area of 239 square miles, and the capital is Kingstown. The language spoken is English. The most southern limit of this territory was Rapid or Gun Point on Carriacou until 1990. This beautiful windswept peninsula juts out into the dividing channel at a latitude of 12.32° South. The fact that it was nearly part of Grenada, another independent territory, made it impossible for Vincentians or Grenadians to settle there. It was no man's land, and a miniature free port, a tax haven, inhabited by wild goats and sheep. A cannon manned at different times by both French and English still lies in its original position. The northern limits of St Vincent are 13.15° North. The longitudinal limit is 60.56° West.

In 1517 the King of Spain, Charles V, authorised Bartolomé de Las Casas to enter into a trade that would transport more than 5,000,000 men, women and children from the coast of West Africa, between Senegal and Gabon, to the Caribbean. This human suffering was endured for three hundred years, whilst African potentates bartered with European merchants, and decided upon destinies. In 1834 the slave trade was abolished. A new community of free men and women now strongly outnumbered the white planters and their families. The estate owners turned to contract labourers from India. The Portuguese, Lebanese and Syrians established successful businesses, whilst British law and order ruled the land and courts. The Grenadine islands had been sparsely settled by mainly Scottish families, mariners and shipwrights with names like Macintosh, Compton, Stewart, Mulzac, McQuilkin and McLaurence. Their religious tendency was Protestant, and the churches were filled with the hauntingly beautiful songs handed down from their fathers as well as the negro spirituals. The men went to sea and set their nets and fishpots, or angled with hook and line, whilst the women made

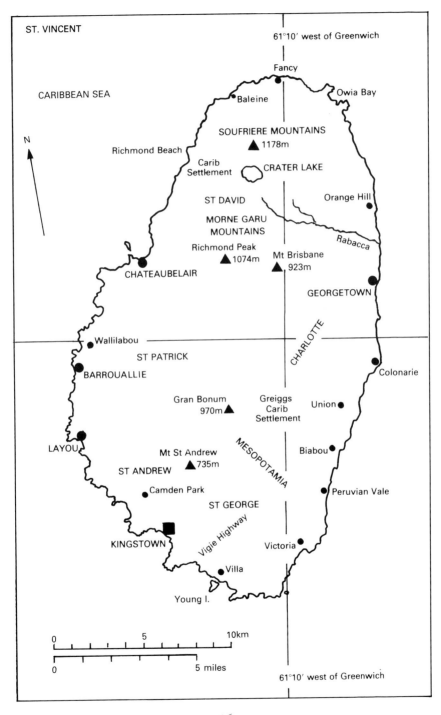

ST. VINCENT

61°10' west of Greenwich

CARIBBEAN SEA

N

Fancy

Owia Bay

Baleine

SOUFRIERE MOUNTAINS
▲ 1178m

Richmond Beach

Carib
Settlement

CRATER LAKE

ST DAVID

Orange Hill

MORNE GARU
MOUNTAINS

Rabacca

Richmond Peak
▲ 1074m

Mt Brisbane
▲ 923m

CHATEAUBELAIR

GEORGETOWN

CHARLOTTE

Wallilabou

ST PATRICK

Colonarie

BARROUALLIE

Gran Bonum
970m ▲

Greiggs
Carib
Settlement

Union

MESOPOTAMIA

LAYOU

Mt St Andrew
▲ 735m

Biabou

ST ANDREW

Camden Park

Peruvian Vale

ST GEORGE

KINGSTOWN

Vigie Highway

Victoria

Villa

Young I.

0   5   10km

0   5 miles

61°10' west of Greenwich

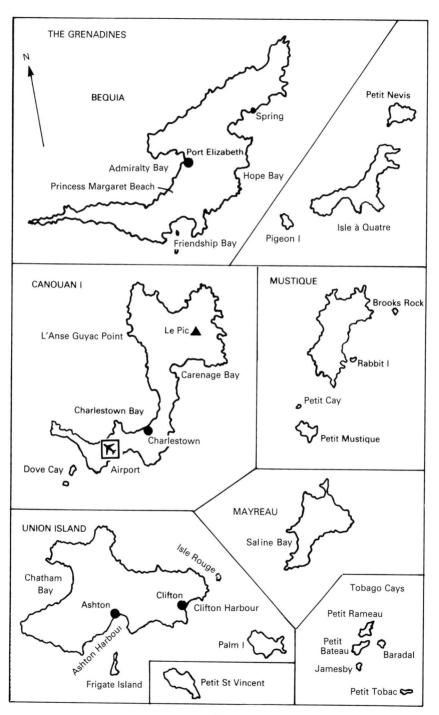

THE GRENADINES

N

BEQUIA

Spring

Petit Nevis

Port Elizabeth

Admiralty Bay

Hope Bay

Princess Margaret Beach

Isle à Quatre

Friendship Bay

Pigeon I

CANOUAN I

L'Anse Guyac Point

Le Pic ▲

Carenage Bay

Charlestown Bay

Charlestown

Dove Cay

Airport

MUSTIQUE

Brooks Rock

Rabbit I

Petit Cay

Petit Mustique

MAYREAU

Saline Bay

UNION ISLAND

Isle Rouge

Chatham Bay

Ashton

Clifton

Clifton Harbour

Ashton Harbour

Palm I

Frigate Island

Petit St Vincent

Tobago Cays

Petit Rameau

Petit Bateau

Baradal

Jamesby

Petit Tobac

17

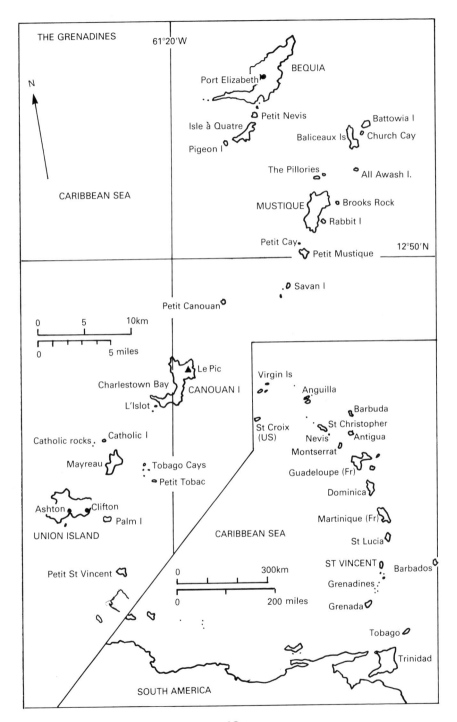

THE GRENADINES

61°20'W

N

CARIBBEAN SEA

BEQUIA

Port Elizabeth

Petit Nevis

Isle à Quatre

Pigeon I

Baliceaux Is

Battowia I

Church Cay

The Pillories

All Awash I.

MUSTIQUE

Brooks Rock

Rabbit I

Petit Cay

Petit Mustique

12°50'N

Savan I

Petit Canouan

0   5   10km

0   5 miles

Le Pic

Charlestown Bay

CANOUAN I

L'Islot

Virgin Is

Anguilla

Barbuda

St Croix
(US)

St Christopher

Nevis

Antigua

Montserrat

Catholic rocks

Catholic I

Guadeloupe (Fr)

Mayreau

Tobago Cays

Petit Tobac

Dominica

Ashton

Clifton

Palm I

UNION ISLAND

Martinique (Fr)

St Lucia

CARIBBEAN SEA

ST VINCENT

Barbados

Petit St Vincent

0   300km

Grenadines

0   200 miles

Grenada

Tobago

Trinidad

SOUTH AMERICA

18

Rosiane from Campbell, a Grenadine beauty (LESLEY SUTTY)

charcoal and cultivated the fields during the rainy season. The shipwrights built sloops and topmasted schooners which traded from north to south, carrying fruits and vegetables, wines and champagne, and later flour and cement for building, as the colony grew.

Mending the fishing net (LESLEY SUTTY)

For many years the country was considered to be the most stable in its politics and government. At the time of independence Prime Minister Milton Cato governed with a socialist assembly.

In 1984 James Mitchell, the leader of the opposition New Democratic Party, was elected to be the country's leader. 'Son', as he was affectionately called by his fellow countrymen, was a Bequia man, passionate and determined. He remained close to his people while responding to ever-changing world situations. He was to create a climate of stability and progress.

| 5 |
The volcano

La Soufriére is the most majestic and energetic volcano of the Caribbean. Major eruptions occurred in 1812, 1902 and 1979. the eruption of 1902 coincided with that of St Pierre in Martinique, which claimed 30,000 lives on that island, and 2000 in St Vincent.

There is ample evidence of volcanic eruptions taking place during the prehistoric era. On Ile de Cailles, an ancient Calivignoid settlement was destroyed during the eleventh century as pottery caught in the molten lava and boulders has remained to testify. There was a cult which sought to appease the volcano god, Yocahu. *Zemis* or three pointed stones were carved into the form of cones and often buried in fields. La Soufrière (from the French word *souffre*) roared and spread its ash and lava from one end of the island to the other each century. After the 1971 eruption an island appeared in the middle of the crater lake. Legend has it that the lake was bottomless. The multiple tremors and explosions that led to the last massive eruption in 1979 ruptured the western flank modifying the shape of the crater yet again. With St Helens in the States, La Soufrière is one of the volcanoes most constantly surveyed by seismic teams.

On the windward coast access to the volcano is via the Rabacca Dry River. Scoria, pumice and gravel slowly choked the water sources here during the nineteenth and twentieth centuries.

A track leads across the beautiful river bed, then turns left through banana plantations, coconut groves and a bamboo forest. Here the hike begins, and a narrow path over ridges and through begonia-filled ravines leads to the lava fields and the summit. For this six-mile ascent raincoats and good shoes are needed, plus a picnic. The last mile is through steep terrain and over wide volcanic boulders. The dry lava bed in between resembles a glacier. Access to the mouth of the crater itself is often on all fours, as the gradient is very steep and it is difficult to keep a foothold in the loose pumice. Also the wind often blows strongly. From this approach, the crater curves *inward*, and those adventurous enough to explore the rim should do so with utmost caution, especially in cloudy conditions. Here we have a formidable Dante's inferno. There is a small primary flora

La Soufrière's lava beds (LESLEY SUTTY)

of moss and fern at this point, with small frogs inhabiting the rivulets created by the high humidity. It is possible either to take the same path back down to Rabacca, or continue via the southern flank on a track leading to Chateaubelair on the leeward coast, which is recommended. In either case this is an all day excursion.

Sam's Taxi Service in Kingstown will organise transport to and from either side of the volcano. (Sam's Taxi Tours Ltd in Kingstown at 456.4338 or 458.4475, fax 456.4233, Bequia 458.3686. He is also available on VHF 68/16, SSB 82940.) Sam is the longest established taxi-driver in the business, catering for yachtsmen, sightseers and adventurers. He will also be sure that an excellent guide is available upon request. Other reliable services are available through Paradise Tours at 458.4001/5545.

The Forestry Division is able to advise you on more adventurous excursions, telephone 456.1111, ext. 321. The tourist Bureau will provide you with full information on recent developments in it's nature programme and may be reached on 457.1502. At the airport look out for one of the most amenable drivers I have had the pleasure of meeting in the West Indies: Vibert De Souza on 456.5781.

The track to the volcano (opposite) (LESLEY SUTTY)

23

| 6 |
Rivers and villages

Evidence of the emergence of St Vincent more than 25,000,000 years ago, during a period of massive volcanic activity, is today most remarkable on the northern coast and the western cliffs which are halted by the Buccament Valley. The island would otherwise have been far smaller, with its boundaries being La Soufrière, Morne Garu Mountains, Mount Brisbane and Mount St Andrew in the south. The Buccament River has its source at Paradise Malone. It is possible to motor as far as Monteiths and Tecy, villages just below Grand Bonum (Grand Bonhomme or Great Man) whose peak reaches 970 metres. On the eastern flank of Grand Bonum are the magnificent Mesopotamia Valley and the Yambou River Gorges.

Mesopotamia is one of earth's paradises. The valley is fertile and verdant, with large plantations of cocoa, bananas, coconuts and breadfruit. Both valleys have trails leading into the rain forests. The St Vincent Forestry Service has established a park at Vermont. The nature trail leads to the Penniston Valley, and a three-mile hike through the forest with helonicas, giant ferns, palms and blue mahos. The rare St Vincent parrot may be sighted here. The river valleys of St Vincent were the first points of human contact, where large social communities developed. Most of the main villages such as Layou, Barrouallie, Arnos Vale-Indian Bay, Yambou and North Union have magnificent petroglyphs, carved on rocks more than 1500 years ago by Indians. Those interested in visiting these sites may be guided by Kirby's small volume *The Petroglyphs of St Vincent* which is available at Kingstown and the Museum.

The drive up the windward highway is spectacular. The Atlantic rollers pound the shores and bathing is not advisable. The coast road from Kingstown via Villa and Stubbs leads to Peruvian and Henry's Vale. The Highway proper starts after the arrowroot factory at Colonarie. The factory is well worth a visit. Leaving Colonarie, which is on a promontory, the road leads through the never-ending beauty of lush tropical vegetation and gardens. The grassy plains of the littoral are unexpected; before continuing it is possible to buy excellent fruit – bananas, soursops, avocado pears and mangoes – at

Washing day (LESLEY SUTTY)

a small isolated shop on the right at the entrance to the highway. The second largest town on the island, Georgetown, has numerous snack bars, a bank, and hospital. There is a small airfield to the north at Rabacca, used mainly by the banana-spraying planes.

The road continues through to Orange Hill. This estate is one of

The Mesopotamia valley (LESLEY SUTTY)

the largest coconut plantations in the world, with 3200 acres of beautifully kept land. The atmosphere is serene and bewitching. In 1986 the Canadians carried out important road works on this end of the island which has improved access considerably. However the road ends on the cliffs of Fancy. Here the village is perched on the hills facing St Lucia. The gingerbread houses are delicately moulded into rich ochre-coloured clay banks.

It is possible to hike the eight miles from Fancy to Richmond beach along the cliffs, via Baleine Falls, leaving early in the morning. This area can otherwise by visited from the leeward coast by chartering a boat and guide. Should you decide to return by the Windward Highway, take time to explore the numerous river valleys and mountain villages. At Peruvian Vale head for Montreal estate via Mesopotamia, where it is possible to buy bouquets of anthuriums, wax roses, heliconias, and other tropical blooms. The estate also has a honeymoon hideaway, a bar and swimming pool. It is known as a spa. The Teviot River whose source is at Grand Bonum just above Montreal runs through the estate, which has been planned around the different streams and brooks branching off from it. Leaving

The Windward Coast (J AND Y BOURVEAU)

Mesopotamia take the Vigie Highway through the interior, which will take you to Arnos Vale and E.T. Joshua airport and on to the capital, Kingstown.

To visit the leeward or west coast of the island it is best to start from Kingstown. The ride is impressive as the steep mountain ridges plunge into the sea, often making the coast inaccessible. There are three main towns on this coast, Layou, Barrouallie and Chateaubelair. Just north of Chateaubelair is Richmond Beach, which has volcanic sands, cool almond trees and excellent fishing. They are all worth visiting.

Beware of undertows at river mouths on this coast. Trinity Falls (with three cascades) just north-east of Richmond Beach are a must. Drive to Ridun and Vale Academy. Turn right at the entrance to the Academy Shop, drive just over 4 km inland and then hike about $3^{1}/_{4}$ km on the rugged trail. A guide is essential and available on request at the Forestry Division.

Montreal Gardens (overleaf) (LESLEY SUTTY)

27

Layou is a mysterious, magical place. The fishermen of Barrouallie still fish for the pilot whale or black fish, and have recently received a donation of modern equipment from Japan for this. The nineteenth century boiling pots for extracting whale oil are still scattered along the beach exactly as they were and are still in use. Chateaubelair is a busy town, rich in history with a wealth of traditional houses. The road ends at Richmond Beach. It is possible to negotiate the charter of a fishing boat on the spot (or book ahead with Baleine Tours at 457.4089) to visit the exceptionally beautiful creeks and bays leading to Baleine Falls, where a natural swimming pool lies below the hundred feet high cascades. The diving is quite spectacular off this part of the coast, with a wealth of crinoids, water lilies, soft and hard corals, crustaceans and reef fish. Many of the larger pelagic (open sea) fish frequently hunt here. This excursion is an absolute must for admirers of marine life and coral gardens. Be sure of sea conditions before you set out with your guide, as at times a ground swell comes down this part of the coast. The water is usually crystal clear. It is impossible to anchor off the coast as the waters are extremely deep.

Leeward Coast of St Vincent (LESLEY SUTTY)

Scuba diving is highly recommended for confirmed divers, and Dive St Vincent (Bill Tewes at 457.4928) at Villa, will help you discover all of these areas. It is strongly recommended that expert services are used, rather than visitors venturing into these areas alone without knowledge of the terrain and total security. Scuba diving is a sport requiring discipline, technique, certification – and much good sense.

Hal and Beverly Daize of Sea Breeze Guest House and Yachts, based at Indian Bay, telephone 458.4969 offer an unique chance to visit the Leeward coast. One not to be missed. Hal has developed an extraordinary understanding with the whale and dolphin populations of St Vincent and has been adopted by several dolphin groups. If you are longing for an encounter with these wonderful ocean inhabitants, a days' excursion with Hal is not to be missed – and for only $US30. You will be able to admire the great beauty of the coastline at the same time. The vessel anchors off the Falls for lunch and snorkeling.

Cumberland Bay and Wallilabou both offer shelter to incoming yachts. However Chatoyer has left his mark quite strongly at Cumberland, and there are rules of propriety regarding the coconut trees and putting out lines. If you do not speak the local dialect you are informed that a fee is levied by the residents, and there is no point refusing to pay the few dollars requested. The bay itself is magnificent, the water deep, however do not anchor overnight at Cumberland Bay. At Wallilabou, leave a watch on board, and raise dinghies at night. Here excellent excursions up the river to the Falls through exotic natural kitchen gardens may be made in the late afternoon under a luminous golden light as the sun sets. It is possible to bathe here in fresh, cool water.

Most yachtsmen anchor off Villa between the jetty and Young Island in the south for maximum security and safety.

Horseshoe Reef, Tobago Cays (overleaf) (CHRIS HUXLEY)

| 7 |
Scuba diving

Throughout this guide a number of very beautiful underwater excursions are mentioned. These areas may be visited either by snorkelling or by use of compressed air units, i.e. scuba tanks. I would, however, like to stress two points, resulting from over twenty years of diving under the surface of the Caribbean Sea and more precisely that of the Grenadines and St Vincent.

The first is the immense beauty of the marine world of this region and the second is the tides and currents which are notoriously strong, both on the surface and the seabed itself, according to equinoxes, moon and month. NEVER underestimate these factors and remember that neap tide (no tide) is either preceded or followed by very strong tides, especially in open waters, on points, and in channels. Be cautious before leaving ship or shore for a swim.

Scuba diving is for certified divers and is best carried out with a monitor who is familiar with sea conditions and tide tables, and is equipped with full security. Decompression chambers, in case of accident, can be reached only by helicopter and the service exists in Martinique and Puerto Rico. The recommended safety depth is 25 metres. Free diving off the shallow coral reefs is by far the most rewarding aquatic activity in this part of the world if not throughout the whole West Indies. There is an unequalled rich marine life in crystalline waters.

| 8 |
The capital, Kingstown

The capital of St Vincent, Kingstown, is often confused with the
capital of Jamaica Kingston (note the lack of a 'w' here). Kingstown
in the south of the island was for years protected by cannons, which
are still here today, but unmanned. Forts Charlotte and Duvernette
were the most heavily fortified. Fort Charlotte is to benefit from
a restoration programme funded by the EEC and the Caribbean
Development Bank (CDB). The National Trust of St Vincent is

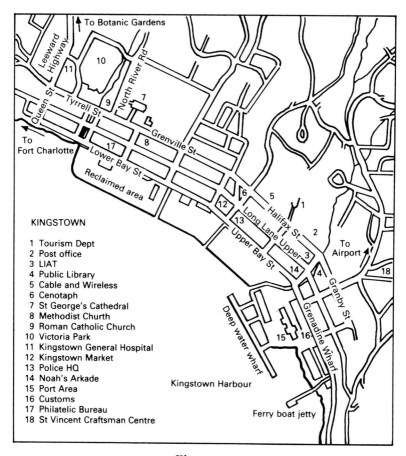

KINGSTOWN

1 Tourism Dept
2 Post office
3 LIAT
4 Public Library
5 Cable and Wireless
6 Cenotaph
7 St George's Cathedral
8 Methodist Church
9 Roman Catholic Church
10 Victoria Park
11 Kingstown General Hospital
12 Kingstown Market
13 Police HQ
14 Noah's Arkade
15 Port Area
16 Customs
17 Philatelic Bureau
18 St Vincent Craftsman Centre

Kingstown

Fort Charlotte (J AND Y BOURVEAU)

extremely active in the conservation of its cultural heritage, and welcomes members. The President is Lavinia Gunn of Noah's Arkade in Bay Street. Each of the Grenadine islands had a fort with multiple batteries placed strategically north and south. Fort Hamilton on Bequia is worth visiting.

Do not be surprised if you come across a cannon when you hike through the bush; some of these have rolled down the hills over the years. Some of these cannons were taken away as souvenirs, despite their great weight. This is against the law, and can involve a prison sentence.

Kingstown has a series of shaded Georgian arcades and cobblestone streets, which make shopping there a pleasant pastime. The main shopping areas are Bay Street on the front, and Middle Street. A cool nineteenth century alley divides the two streets at the level of Cobblestone Inn, which is a favourite meeting place for most Vincentians and travellers. The hotel has excellent facilities with colonial furnishings in most of the bedrooms. Basil Charles of Mustique fame has taken over the restaurant and meals are generous and well-prepared. There is a buffet at lunchtime.

At the northern end of Bay Street you will find the market. There is a very wide selection of tropical fruits and vegetables transported

A Kingstown house (LESLEY SUTTY)
A shoe shop in Kingstown (J AND Y BOURVEAU)

from the outlying villages each day. There is also a charcoal market facing the new fish market. Coconuts are sold from barrows while they are still green with soft delicious jelly. The vendors deftly open these large young nuts with three quick and well-placed blows of the cutlass. The water of these coconuts is both refreshing and excellent for the health. Prices are highly competitive and this is one of the best places in the Caribbean for yachtsmen to take provisions on board.

In 1970 the waterfront was expanded, and a dredging programme was undertaken to provide additional container space and room for two freighters or cruise ships to come alongside. The main dock is at the south end of Kingstown. This is where the ferries come in from the Grenadines. It is also possible to anchor to the right of the dock when taking on provisions. Water is available at the commercial dock, on request at the customs house. For a minimal fee it is possible to fill tanks before leaving for the Grenadines where supplies are rare. This manoeuvre can, however, call for a show of steely nerves. Thirty-five per cent of the population are unemployed, and much of the youth converges on the capital and its port. Some of these youths are belligerent, establishing their own laws and rights when officials turn their backs. Be patient, this is not the general

The market, Kingstown (LESLEY SUTTY)

rule. Very small boys have home-made wooden carts to carry ice, supermarket goods, and anything you may have bought for a cruise. It is well worthwhile giving them a few dollars to carry your crates and goods, see them smile widely and know you have a friend here.

Two excellent supermarkets function directly behind the main jetty. The meat is first-class and local. Customs and immigrations offices are located here. An immigration/permit office is situated at the end of Bay Street.

There are some very old and interesting traditional buildings on the waterfront of the southern anchorage. The diving is good in this area. Please keep to the rocky shore.

The centre of town has a number of banks, restaurants, bars, the post office and the government administrative buildings on Halifax Street. For philatelists the stamps of St Vincent and the Grenadines are collector's items. There is a philatelic club in town. Kingstown closes its doors to commerce at 4 p.m. and for lunch between 12 and 1 p.m. Opening hours vary between 7 a.m. for essential services, and 9 a.m. for shoppers. Shopping for spare parts is not advised. Bring these with you. A good breakfast is served from eight in the morning at the Green Parrot on Halifax Street, when Cable and Wireless opens up on the other side of the street. Service here is efficient for both telephone and fax. Laundry is dealt with in a happy tropical atmosphere at the Black Cat Laundry at the far end of Long Lane.

There are three churches in Kingstown. The Catholic Cathedral, St Mary's, is an extraordinary structure and gothic in style. St Mary's was built in 1823 and was renovated in 1940 by Charles Verbeke. A short distance from it is St George's Anglican Cathedral, built in 1820. It is light, airy and Georgian in style. This church has fine stained glass windows. The Methodist church is also attractive and merits a visit; it is only a stone's throw from the other two.

Dollar buses operate from the market place and in front of the town's handsome Court House. These colourful public transport vehicles service all the villages on both the leeward and windward coasts. There is a busy service between Kingstown and the tourist centre at Villa, which goes past the airport.

Before leaving town it is very worthwhile to visit the oldest Botanical Garden in the Western Hemisphere. It is here that Captain Bligh planted the first Tahitian breadfruit tree in 1793. A slip from it carries on the tradition in the gardens. The gardens were opened

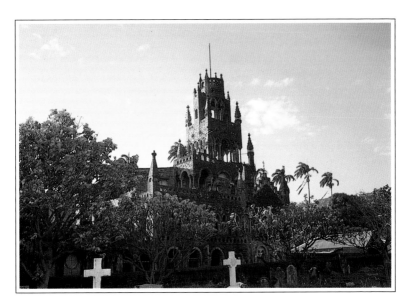

St Mary's Catholic Cathedral (J AND Y BOURVEAU)

in 1765 on twenty acres of rich and fertile soil on the slopes
overlooking the capital. The first botanists to cultivate the gardens,
Drs George Young and Alexander Anderson, were responsible for
the propagation of numerous imported flowering shrubs, plants and
trees, both decorative and medicinal, throughout the island. The
success of the breadfruit trees provided the people with an excellent
food source. There are fine royal palms and just about every species
of Caribbean fruit, flower, shrub and tree may be studied here. A
Doric temple was added to the grounds at the beginning of the
century together with paths and shaded benches, where visitors can
sit and admire the beauty and enjoy the tranquillity of the place.

Above the gardens is the Botanical Clinic founded by a dedicated
general surgeon Dr Cecil Cyrus. Dr Cyrus is also responsible for the
Ophthalmological Centre where over the years he has solved many
critical problems. The clinics look over the town and Kingstown
harbour.

Another of the island's remarkable men also works in this area.
Within the Botanical Gardens is the Archaeological Museum founded
by Dr Earl Kirby. Dr Kirby received the Caribbean Conservation
Association Award for Outstanding Services to the region in 1991.
Not only is he a historian, archaeologist and author, he is also a

The Botanic Gardens (J AND Y BOURVEAU)

veterinary surgeon and has worked in the fields, villages, mountains and towns of the State, aware of every aspect of its fauna and flora. His museum is a charming gingerbread house on the left of the entrance. Open on Wednesday from 9.45 a.m. to 11.45 a.m. and Saturday from 4 p.m. to 6 p.m., the exhibition traces the lives of the

The lily pond in the Botanic Gardens (J AND Y BOURVEAU)

41

prehistoric settlers of the island, displaying magnificent artefacts, stone and shell tools.

It is worth stopping at the Craftsmen Centre on the way out of town for Villa and the tourist section of St Vincent. There is an excellent selection of handicrafts here, including wood carvings, sisal mats and rugs, which may be made to order, and a variety of bamboo ware, straw hats and worked coconuts.

The Government encourages foreign investment in both tourism and industry. The recent Hotel Aid Act drawn up by the Prime Minister seeks to encourage economic growth in this field. Serious investors may contact The Development Corporation at P.O. Box 841, St Vincent and the Grenadines, W.I. Finally, for those wishing to start married life in paradise, aliens and tourists may obtain a Special Governor General Licence for a small fee from the Ministry of Information and Culture, after a three-day residence in the State, and an Ordinary Licence from the Registrar. Notice of the ceremony has to be published in the registry for a minimum of seven days. The choice of honeymoon hideaways will prove overwhelming.

| 9 |
Villa, Young Island and Calliaqua

E.T. Joshua Airport is now equipped for night landing. The rugged topography of St Vincent, which makes it unique, has not allowed for an airstrip that can cope with the heavy transporters, like 747s and DC10s. A late-night ferry runs from St Vincent to the island of Bequia at 7 p.m. The small airport on Bequia now functions occasionally. Flight schedules for Bequia are available from E.T. Joshua Airport, telephone 456.5610.

Villa, Indian Bay and Young island are the gateway to the Grenadine Islands, with a first-class choice of hotels, inns, and apartments for those who wish to explore St Vincent.

The first bareboat charter company (yachts equipped and provisioned for use by experienced crews) in the Caribbean was established at Calliaqua by Caribbean Sailing Yachts in 1970. CSY has since built a hotel and provided skippers for holidaymakers wishing to go to sea and learn. The passage out of Calliaqua lagoon is very narrow, but well-marked. If in doubt the company will send an outboard to guide you. The service stands by on VHF 68 and 16, also 86.

The most extravagant and luxurious resort is on the historic Young Island, 200 yards off the jetty at Villa. Part of this haven is the rock known as Fort Rock or Fort Duvernette, which still boasts its original cannons and mortars used during the numerous skirmishes between the French and the England. The resort organises barbecues and visits to the Fort. Access is by boat. Young Island is a magnificent mixture of exotic tropical flowers and palms, pools and colourful birds, with beautiful coral gardens off the pure white sands. For amateur tasters of rum punch and exotic cocktails, Young Island offers the best to be had. There is often a calypso orchestra there in the evening at sunset.

The bungalows have their own patios all with breathtaking views. Yachts anchoring in the channel here (Villa-Young Island) are warned that the tide is fickle and boats can rotate a full 360° on

Villa-Calliaqua (overleaf) (LESLEY SUTTY)

43

their anchors. Give your neighbour ample space; this can avoid inconveniences of humour. Bathers should **not** try to cross from the mainland to Young Island as the tide, as mentioned, is unpredictable. A small ferry runs back and forth between Young Island and the jetty on the mainland day and night. There are a number of first class restaurants at Villa. The Mariners Inn and the French Restaurant founded by the Despointes family, are favourite meeting places for yachtsmen, tourists and anyone wishing to enjoy an excellent evening out. The bar at Mariners is a work of art, and the atmosphere is enhanced by excellent music.

The diving between Fort Duvernette and the southern side of Young Island is rewarding. There is a wide variety of nudibranch or sea slugs, willing to reveal their feathery beauty. Do not try to dive off the windward side of the reef dividing Fort Duvernette from Young Island, unless accompanied by a security boat. There are strong rip tides for vessels beating upwind from Kingstown Harbour to Young Island and the Bequia Channel.

Nine miles separate St Vincent from the largest of its dependencies, Bequia.

| 10 |
St Vincent coast guard

Two extremely efficient coast guard vessels are stationed in Calliaqua, *The Captain Mulzac* and *The George Macintosh*. These ships stand by twenty-four hours a day on VHF channels 16 and 68 and are assisted by a very capable group of radio operators at St Vincent Signal Station based at Fort Charlotte. In a State where its dependencies are isolated, and its yachting community, tourists and working vessels are constantly in need of assistance, manoeuvres are carried out on a daily basis. Intense traffic is dealt with in transmitting messages to tankers, cruise ships, and all seafarers and their families on land. The Grenadine barrier reefs are dangerous, and any vessel in distress should immediately contact the signal station or coast guard, whose call signs are those given here. Advice will be given and assistance forthcoming. Hesitation in contacting these stations has caused loss of life and vessels in the area. Do not be surprised if you are asked to repeat a number of times your position, description of vessel and persons on board. Ask other vessels to relay for you if necessary. Remain on stand-by on Channel 16 for as long as you are in distress, unless requested by the authorities to change to another frequency. Motorised vessels suffering from a breakdown of the main engines should be aware of the westerly current and wind direction that will quickly blow them out of hearing distance or radio range. Fishing yawls have been relocated off Guadeloupe recently, after three weeks drifting, in the first place, off St Vincent. Vessels have also been recovered off the coast of Venezuela. The greatest danger is failure of small outboard motors on annex dinghies. These craft shift quickly out to sea and are lost in the swells. Be sure to carry oars and sufficient line and anchor.

The reasons for these recommendations is that over the past twenty years distress calls have increased. The coast guard tries to educate all seafarers and minimise the dangers. An air-sea rescue operation is a very costly business.

| 11 |
Agriculture, pests and flora

St Vincent's economy relies on the well-being of its agriculture. Volcanic eruptions, tropical storms and hurricanes have through the centuries devastated banana crops, plantations of coconuts, cocoa and many species of fruits and vegetables. The Banana Growers' Association organises the weekly supply by farmers of the agreed quota which is sold. Some 60,000 tonnes are transported each year to England on regional freighters; 45% of the banana crop is grown on the east coast. The country benefited from EEC status as an Overseas Territory until 1979, when upon independence it acceded to the Lomé Conventions. The Single European Market is of considerable concern to the Windward Islands and St Vincent as the preferential sale of bananas to the European Union is in the balance.

The nectar-eating bat and the hornet 'Jack the Spaniard' help to pollinate the banana crops. The tiny bat is not shy and often observed on its nighttime rounds. On the other hand the fruit-eating bat will quickly locate a bunch of ripe bananas in a kitchen or hanging from the stern of a ship. These bats choose ripe fruit, and are also fond of paw paw. They are elusive creatures well worth waiting for.

Large ECU grants have been designated by the EEC to assist in the diversification of crops, land reform and the development of the Orange Hill Estate. Some eighty farmers signed leases for plots of land, and have started to plant sweet potatoes, eddoes, peppers, cabbage, tomatoes, paw paw, pineapple and citrus.

The African desert locust whirled across the Atlantic in great clouds, forerunners to Hurricane Joan, in 1987. The world at large remained disbelieving, as this was the first such migration in history. Most of these insects arrived in a state of exhaustion. An eradication programme was enforced. Some isolated species survived in the dry

A banana tree (opposite) (LESLEY SUTTY)

Pineapples, a newly introduced crop (J AND Y BOURVEAU)

sandy conditions of the southern Grenadines. It is possible that they may have crossbred with the indigenous Giant Brown Cricket *Tropidacris dux*, which it closely resembles in form. The African desert locust is salmon coloured with turquoise eyes, easily distinguishable from the former.

The farmer's nightmare is the biting black ant colonies, which devour crops, shrubs and trees. They have a preference for citrus trees and pigeon pea bushes. The ant has powerful mandibles, hanging on hard as it bites. Worms and other parasites, together with land crabs, have made the cultivation of potatoes (although of American origin) impossible.

There are government spray programmes for both ants and the mosquito *Aedis aegyptii*, which is a carrier of the dengue fever virus. It is a serious enough virus to merit hospitalisation. Symptoms are high fever (105-106°F), head and joint pains, followed by a rash and intense itching. Aspirin and Vitamin C are the only known cure; there is no vaccine.

The different varieties of mangoes are in season from March to August, when the avocado pear comes into season. Agriculture in the Grenadines is restricted to and governed by rainfall. White sweet potatoes, a prized root crop, are planted in sand during November, together with red sweet potatoes. Peas are perennial and can resist drought for years. Sweet corn is a hazardous crop, planted annually. The failure percentage is high, and the small farmers are slowly abandoning its cultivation. Guava and Jamaica and Bequia plums are surprisingly hardy and bear from one dry season to the next. During the eighteenth and nineteenth centuries cotton was planted in the Grenadines and was its first source of income. Sea island cotton is the finest in the world, silky and long-lasting. The Stevenson family from England settled at Wallilabou on St Vincent in the 1960s and were the pioneers of the batik trade on the island. They produced extravagant brilliantly coloured cloth. The Stevenson batik became world famous and the original works are collector's items. Sea island cotton is a rare commodity today, although the batik trade has developed considerably.

St Vincent is the largest producer of arrowroot. The rhizomes are laboriously cultivated, harvested and transformed into a very fine starch, used for cooking and more recently as a dressing for computer paper.

A local radio programme 'Grass Roots' is broadcast for the benefit of the small farmers on subjects of interest, importance and understanding which will allow them to deal with the numerous incidental, minor or major disturbances caused by parasites, insects, fungi, soil, humidity or drought.

Flora

The different species of mango, banana – the favoured bluggoe and the plantain – and avocado pear originate from flowers and end up as fruits and vegetables according to the degree of ripeness. Most tropical fruits can be used green as a vegetable. The true flora is represented by increasing varieties of the jewel coloured single, double, and triple hibiscus; the hardiest exotic shrub is the bougainvillea. Most of the women are keen gardeners. Ixoria, red, salmon and pink, frangipani, oleander, allamanda, together with the many flowering trees such as the flamboyant and yellow poui are the most cooperative. Nearly all of the ornamental flowers and shrubs were imported from Asia and the Pacific. The coconut tree came from Africa. Most shrubs have a cultural significance. Many of the wild flowers, their berries and seeds, are highly toxic. The manchineel tree, which is a particularly useful soil retainer along

Heliconia (LESLEY SUTTY)   **Cotton** (LESLEY SUTTY)

Copra (LESLEY SUTTY)

the shore, has a highly poisonous, sweet smelling golden green apple, the size of a silver dollar. The milky sap is equally dangerous. You should not stand under the tree when it rains, but can certainly benefit from its shade when the sun shines. These precious forests of manchineel are being critically endangered due to development. As the trees disappear the beach fronts erode, and the many animal, bird and insect species that live in the bowers and roots lose their habitats. A companion tree which bears handsome bunches of edible grapes, rich in vitamin C, is the seagrape tree. The fruit ripens in October. The tree is equally under threat. The leaves are glossy and round, and once shed, carpet the land with rich bronze colours. Both of these useful trees have quality wood; in the case of the manchineel the wood has to dry for some years, and burning fresh logs should be avoided as the smoke will blister the skin and is highly irritant for both eyes and lungs. Both trees are indigenous. There is a very nasty stinging plant, the burn bush, which has made the Grenadines its stronghold. The small white flowers, stems and large vine shaped leaves are covered with multiple nematocysts, or fine glassy spikes that will puncture and cling to the skin, leaving many small wounds. The rash quickly evolves into ugly red lumps. Fortunately you can nearly always be sure to find the medicinal aloe plant nearby. The long smooth fleshy leaves are rich in a pungent Bovril-smelling gelatine. This substance is applied to every type of burn; as it dries it makes a natural compress, and rapidly soothes. The most precious trees found on the islands are teak and mahogany. The gommier is often used for boatbuilding.

| 12 |
Fauna

The Forestry Service safeguards and protects its rich environment, the nation's children participate actively in awareness programmes promoted by the National Trust and the Eastern Caribbean Coalition for Environmental Awareness. High up in the tropical rainforest, the island's national parrot 'Vincie' flies through the air. Fines for the collection or hunting of this bird are some EC$2000 and a prison sentence. A breeding programme is in process at the Botanical Gardens. There are few indigenous animals. These include the now rare armadillo, agouti and manicou-marsupial. All of them are shy forest and bush dwellers in need of definitive protection. The government has taken steps in this direction by establishing nature reserves and closed seasons during the breeding periods.

A manicou (LESLEY SUTTY)

**Pilot Whales swimming close to shore,
leeward of St Vincent** (COURTESY I.F.A.W.)

There is a strong enforcement of closed seasons for turtles, lobster and white sea urchin, year round. The articles of these laws are on display at customs, immigration and post offices. The fines run as high as EC$5000 for an offence, and confiscation of material. A closed season for the endangered queen conch is in force. Spear fishing is prohibited in the State. Unlawful fishing can be punished by fines of up to EC$5000 and three months in prison.

The Grenadines were home to colonies of the large reptilian land iguana. Their numbers have been widely depleted over the past twenty years. The animals are now protected.

The Grenadine seabirds have fortunately been protected by a government Bird Protection Act for some twenty years. This has saved the remaining pelican and boobie bird colonies. The largest seabird nesting sites are the windward cliffs of Baliceaux and Battowia in the north of Mustique. Access to both islands and these breeding grounds is very hazardous. Other breeding grounds are Petit Canouan and Sail Rock. The magnificent man-o-war or frigate bird with its nine feet wingspan can be seen gliding high in the sky on air currents or following fishing vessels, together with the

Sperm Whales and calves; a whale-watcher's dream (COURTESY I.A.F.W.)

laughing gulls. Both of these families are poor fishers, inclined to scavenge and steal. The frigate will harass and claw the agile, sleek boobie, in mid air, until it relinquishes its catch. There are two pairs of nesting ospreys or sea eagles in the Grenadines. These birds of prey may be seen scooping fish from the water off Union Island. Union Island also has the rare cocorico or rufous guan, a pheasant-like bird with a loud chant. This species is known to live in Trinidad and Tobago and Union. It is absent from the other islands. There are many interesting vagrant bird species passing through the Grenadines in March and November, from the Venezuelan swallow-tailed fly catcher, scarlet oriole, great heron, Cuban eagle to the gay, playful swallows migrating across the Atlantic, carried by the high and low air currents which bounce off the 3000 miles of swells between the coast of Africa and the Caribbean. Upon arrival they are often seen to be exhausted. To close my shutters at night I have lifted the birds from their perches and put them elsewhere, without waking them. The younger birds would often sleep for two days before engaging in their favourite sport of 'wind-rushing' off the cliffs. The colonies line up and gather maximum speed on the wing, flying to windward on the northern peninsulas. When wind contact is at its maximum the birds flip over and let the elements push their light bodies back to the starting point. This is the only place in the world I have seen swallows play this game.

White-rumped sandpipers resting on a piece of driftwood (LESLEY SUTTY)

The glossy cow bird is also a vagrant, whose song is startling, varying between rushing water and the song of the lark, which is enough to encourage anyone living in a drought-stricken area to leave his home. I was tricked. I looked for the source of this sound for some time before the variable pretty song of this bird returned to normal. They have the bad habit of taking over other birds' nests, in much the same way as the European cuckoo. The call of the crested night heron may have you intrigued. This wide billed, plump grey bird has a black crest and white band through the eye. He looks very much like Donald Duck. Living in mangrove forests, he is as curious as he is shy. The Grenadine islands have large areas of mangrove bordering shores behind the windward coast barrier reefs. Wildlife here is fascinating, and numerous lizard, crab and bird species may be observed.

The humming bird and bananaquit quickly become part of a household and establish their nests in plants, lamps and baskets. Many of the smaller bird species nest in the ever multiplying cacti and thorn bushes, where they are amply protected from snakes, other birds and man. Coca-Cola is a favourite with both small birds and lizards if you wish to observe them at close quarters.

| 13 |
Traditional architecture

Kingstown has many handsome Georgian buildings and two-storey gingerbread houses. Usually the ground floor is constructed in stone and cement masonry with decorative wrought iron balconies , or gingerbread fretwork dividing the living areas of the upper levels. These are always colourfully decorated with lozenges, hearts, rosettes and imaginative carvings, painted in rich colours. The stone buildings known as 'Great Houses' were the original estate houses in the outlying villages. The Orange Hill Great House has remained intact, whilst many others are now romantic ruins, devastated by hurricanes. The modest chattel house or salt box dwelling was a standard board house measuring 26×28 feet, divided into four rooms, with an outside kitchen, water closet and water tank. These were designed for maximum aeration with exquisite fretwork throughout, influenced by Victorian designs. Built on stilts, the houses were easily transportable. The estates usually had their own

A traditional chattel house in the Grenadines (LESLEY SUTTY)

carpenters and ebenists, and the four-poster beds, consoles and sofas were the hallmark of each island. Today many of the old bedposts have been relegated to fence posts and the population opts for modern furniture. The government encourages hurricane-proof cement block houses. The men are gifted masons using the local

A house built from wattle and daub (LESLEY SUTTY)

iron-stone and blue bitch which is a small industry throughout the Grenadines. There are a number of quarries, where for a minimum wage, men, women and children chip stone.

Shingle-covered board houses were first built in the nineteenth century. The wooden tiles added strength and beauty to the plain structures. Wattle and daub huts can still be seen in the remoter villages, though the thatched roofs are now so rare that their preservation as part of our cultural heritage is urgent.

The ruins of an 18th century sugar factory (LESLEY SUTTY)

| 14 |
Folklore and music

The Caribs passed on a wealth of tales, superstitions and medicinal cures to their descendants. Many of these medicinal cures had been used for centuries by their forebears. These in time were modified by the West African cultures.

The night spirits or 'jumbies' start their activities at sunset. In the more isolated areas of the dependencies villagers still shut out all of these mischievous beings by hermetically closing their doors and windows at night. If they must 'travel abroad' after dark, they will do so with a supply of tobacco in their pockets, which is considered highly protective. The women wear their underwear inside out, and use their skirts as a shield to reflect the light. The 'jumby' has no shadow; it can at will adopt many human and animal forms. The female witch 'Cocomar' can best be delayed from entering a home by placing a heap of fine sand on the doorstep. She must count each grain before crossing the threshold, and this task can take until sunrise when she has to leave.

It is common to see livestock, especially sheep, with red ribbons round their necks. The villagers themselves will also dress only in red when a malevolent neighbour has set a curse or cast a spell on them and their animals. The cattle that wear these ribbons do so in many cases to prevent the devil taking on their form or making use of them. To deflect evil, black beads are treasured and considered highly protective when sewn inside clothing together with other talismans. Spurned lovers often turn to sorcery, at the same time loudly advertising a partner's misdemeanours on the streets. The psychological pressure in both cases is highly effective.

Carnival is the time when the familiar troops of devils and angels give battle. All of them dress in flamboyant costumes sparkling with sequins, clusters of feathers and silks. Special teams beat their way through the streets, striking walls, floors and trees, and finally a well-padded player or players launch into battle. The true meaning of Carnival, or Mardi Gras, during Carême is often forgotten. Both the religious and superstitious character of this festival were promoted to remind the population of the suffering of Christ.

A carnival costume, showing part of a wonderful skirt (LESLEY SUTTY)

Modern-day Carnival, although still highly traditional, usually takes place in July in St Vincent and the Grenadines, as the Windward Islands endeavour to rotate this colourful event throughout the year. Carnival became fashionable during the early part of the century in St Vincent. Today the election of the Carnival Queen involves the sponsoring of candidates by hotel resorts and businesses, and the election of the Calypso King. In the field of agriculture, a crown is given to the most industrious male and female worker.

In the Grenadines, and at the close of the dry season, January, February and March, a 'Let Go' season is enforced. This permits goats, sheep and cows to wander freely through the islands, in order to fend for themselves, in a bid for survival. Most of these animals run to the bush, but some remain close to the villages, feeling a certain attachment to their owners. Lawfully all crops must be securely fenced. Should a stray animal plunder the crops, it is captured and tied to a post, where it will be deprived of shade, water and feed for eight days, or until the owner pays for damages. The animal's suffering is enormous, and the owner more than hesitant, aware that the costs will be highly exaggerated. The unclaimed animal's throat is then slit and it is thrown into the dusty road, where no one will touch the body. This severe retribution is usually directed at the many errant, destructive and cunning goats. The custom is slowly dying out.

A more romantic ceremony is the Rain Dance, which is organised when drought has severely menaced the people's well being. A big drum is placed on a promontory and chants and dances imploring the skies to open are performed through the night. There is an astonishing percentage of success, and torrential rains often arrive next day!

Funerals usually conform to the deceased's wishes, and are colourful events with a party afterwards. The small cemeteries are usually on the shore, in the shade of palms; the tombs face out towards the lagoons and reefs. These are beautiful, peaceful resting places, which become bustling, candlelit theatres on the eve of All Saints' Day. Each tomb, lit by dozens of candles, provides a place for a picnic, for the youngest child to the oldest member of the family who keep their ancestors company until midnight.

Music

Calypso songs, often highly political in intent, are a unique form of expression particular to the Windward Islands. These lyrical songs succeeded the sweet negro spirituals of the nineteenth and early

A steel band playing in Kingstown, St Vincent (LESLEY SUTTY)

twentieth century. The Vincentian and Grenadine population are music crazy, and rhythmic from the cradle to the tomb. Steel pan bands became very popular after the war. This unique form of music has now been recognised internationally, with recent homage to it made by the great French musician Jean-Michel Jarre at an open-air concert in Paris, attended by thousands. You should not leave the islands without having heard such an orchestra. Most resorts have a steel band playing on barbecue night. Reggae became popular in the early seventies with Bob Marley. The Shake orchestras with the hand-made calabash, bamboo, violin and guitar music are most colourful. You may have to go into the countryside and smaller localities to hear this music. The players also shuffle dance.

Jazz lovers should go to the Attic in downtown Kingstown. International artists play here.

| 15 |
Seafarers

The Ciboneys in their coracles, and the Arawaks and Caribs in their great dugouts paddled up wind to the islands. Caravelles set out from Europe and small sloops and brigantines carried the first missionaries and settlers from one Caribbean island to the next. For five hundred years men, slaves, animals and freight travelled this way. At the beginning of this century a thriving boatbuilding trade was established on the islands of Bequia and Carriacou in the Grenadines. Handsome top-masted schooners were built, without any plan other than rough sketches in taverns.

Considered the finest sailing grounds in the Caribbean, the coral reefs of the Grenadine archipelago caused many a ship to founder. Vessels trading out of the dependencies, between Florida and Trinidad, succumbed to heavy seas, storms and squalls. Most families have a story to tell of shipwreck, loss of life and rescue from one generation to the next. The strong prevailing easterly Trade Winds, and the unpredictable currents, often seem to plot to make seas froth

'Ruby C.' the last of the Caribbean's Top Masted schooners, built in the Grenadines (LESLEY SUTTY)

and come to life. Only fools sail at night around the barrier reefs of the Grenadines.

Great caution must be exercised as the windward barrier reef of these islands is nearly continuous over the ninety miles of the archipelago it protects. Bays and beaches frequently have a fringing coral reef which can be distinguished by a change of colour in the

A schooner under construction (opposite) (LESLEY SUTTY)

A 'double-ender', St Vincent (LESLEY SUTTY)

The launching (LESLEY SUTTY)

water, from blue or turquoise to brown or yellow. Waves do not always break over these coral heads.

The most frequented anchorages have marker buoys indicating passes and entrance to anchorages. Sometimes these break free and drift out of alignment. You should compare their positions with those noted on the marine charts. The following areas are hazardous and extreme care should be exercised when approaching them.

1 Bequia Rock on the north-east coast of Bequia, heading for Mustique. Heavy rip tides and strong westerly currents result in high seas, with breaking waves. Do not on any account sail close to this rock. The safer route to Mustique is down the lee of Bequia, via Isle à Quatre.

2 The passages between both north and south of Petit Nevis are narrow with strong tides and are not recommended.

3 The Montezuma Shoal to the west of Mustique: Brittania Bay should be approached from the north.

4 The entrance to Charlestown Bay, on the west coast of Canouan: keep close to the left or port side of the black marker buoy.

5 Baline Rock south-west of Canouan and north of the Tobago Cays.

6 Low coral heads south-west of Jamesby Tobago Cays on 12.37° west and 63.42° north.

7 Mayero: Tarzan or Grand Col Point: the reef extends a quarter of a mile from the point; the red marker buoy is known to shift. Keep well outside it.

8 The barrier reef running from the airstrip of Union Island to the entrance of Clifton Harbour. Be sure to leave the three marker buoys to starboard or right. Pass between the third marker buoy and the red flashing marker buoy towards the jetty. Keep west of the inner reef or Monkey Cay; anchor behind the barrier reef.

9 Grand Cay mid-way between Palm Island and Union. The red marker buoy is positioned on the western extremity of this long reef which heads east.

10 Petit St Vincent: the pass is south of Mopion and the north of Pinaise sand bank.

You are advised to hoist dinghies and outboard motors aboard at night to avoid theft. If you have dinner ashore, leave a watch on board.

| 16 |
Bequia and Petit Nevis

Bequia is the largest island of the St Vincent Grenadines. The main anchorage is at Admiralty Bay and the capital of this island, Port Elizabeth. Yachts should anchor to the south of the main jetty, keeping clear of the ferry traffic and, close to shore, the beach shelves steeply to seven and fifteen metres. A sand bank divides this bay from the second anchorage, Princess Margaret Bay. Here it is wise to anchor in the north of the bay; there is ground swell in the south. The sand bank is an interesting area to explore with a mask, whilst both the north and south entrances to these bays have excellent diving, both scuba or snorkelling.

The island is in the throes of major development, with renovation of road surfaces. James Mitchell Airport at Pagets Farm is now in service on the south coast. The main jetty has been extended to cope with the increase in ferry services. An attractive covered market with provisions and handicrafts was recently opened by the Prime Minister.

Port Elizabeth is a charming village. The beaches are covered with pink and white Madagascar periwinkles. Most of the shops are on the waterfront, also the customs, police and immigration offices, where most yachtsmen complete their formalities upon entering and leaving the State. There are benches and a beautiful coconut grove.

Water, ice and fuel are available on the Bequia slip; only small vessels are able to dry dock here. There is also a pleasant bar and restaurant looking out over the water.

Access to the island, though, is mainly by ferry. The service has been greatly improved, with an evening crossing leaving Kingstown jetty at 7 p.m. which enables overseas visitors coming in from Europe and the U.S. via Barbados to make Bequia in one day.

The oldest and certainly favourite rendezvous is the Frangipani Hotel and restaurant owned by James Mitchell. It was once a private home, loft and storage room for the largest schooner built on Bequia, the *Gloria Colita*, owned and skippered by Reginald Mitchell. One of the many mysteries of ships, the Bermuda Triangle, was to be the fate of this lovely schooner. In 1940 the ship was found drifting without trace of her crew, in this strange zone.

Port Elizabeth, Bequia (LESLEY SUTTY)

Many other magnificent schooners were built throughout the years on the shores of Port Elizabeth. The last of the two-masted gaff-rigged schooners built here was *Water Pearl*, for the singer Bob Dylan.

The last of the true top-masted schooners was *Ruby C.* on which I lived and sailed for 14 years. *Ruby C.*, although based in the St

71

Vincent Grenadines, was built by the shipwrights of Carriacou, the Comptons at Windward, in 1948.

There is an excellent choice of restaurants and hotels on the shores of Port Elizabeth, which include the Old Fig Tree and Sunny Caribee which, with the Frangipani, are the oldest establishments. The Frangipani has an orchestra and barbecue on Thursday nights. It is advisable to reserve first. On leaving town head north on the beautiful rambling hilly road that goes to Spring, Industry and Park Estates in that order. The road winds from one coconut grove to the next. At the end of Spring Beach, you will find Carib grinding stones. This whole area was once settled by Amerindians. The most intact remaining estate is Spring, which is a haven of peace. Some twelve rooms are available for those who wish to get away from the crowd. There is a delightful swimming pool with old stone walkways bordered by masses of exotic flowers. This is the oldest working estate in the Grenadines, with a busy copra industry, established more than two hundred years ago. A tennis court is situated between the cool banana plantations and the piles of waiting coconuts. This is a natural, informal and comfortable hideaway.

Spring Estate, Bequia (opposite) (LESLEY SUTTY)

Industry Estate, Bequia (LESLEY SUTTY)

There is an excellent hike to Bullet Point, beyond Park Farm. The path ends near impressive cliffs, pounded by waves, where the air is full of spinning seabirds. Returning in the direction of Port Elizabeth turn left at the crossroads and visit Hope Bay; the views of Mustique, Baliceaux and Battowia are magnificent from here. Mount Pleasant in the south was once the site of an old Fort. This has been restored and is now a delightful hotel and restaurant. It is well worth returning to town to visit the Friendship Bay Resort and Pagets Farm. This is a stone's throw from the island of Petit Nevis, the whaling station. St Vincent claimed aboriginal subsistence whaling rights at the 1990 International Whaling Commission, which she was granted. The Commission gave the chief harpooner Athneal Ollivierre the right to kill three humpback whales each season, December to May, for a period of three years. The hunt is essentially by lateen-rigged sailing vessels and hand harpoons. A whaling museum is in line for the island, as Athneal Ollivierre, now in his seventies, has no eligible successor. Petit Nevis was for the first half of this century the busiest whaling station in the Caribbean. The humpback whales had chosen to breed on the Grenada Bank, waiting for the calves to gain in strength before heading back to the krill grounds where they fed in the North Atlantic. In doing so they attracted the whalers' attentions. American and Norwegian vessels sailed each year from Newfoundland and Nantucket, to harvest the whales. When numbers had been seriously depleted the trade effectively became mechanical on Bequia, and was to remain so.

On return to Port Elizabeth it is worth visiting Hamilton on the north end of Admiralty Bay. Here the Sargeant family build beautiful model boats. These include the whaling boats, local schooners, and famous charter yachts. It is possible to order a replica of your own vessel, which can be packed and sent to you. Boats and boating are an integral part of Bequia. The Regatta held each Easter is an important event, with international participation.

Leaving Bequia by sea (and at the time of writing it is still the best way) and heading south, you will pass in front of a series of original troglodyte houses, built into the cliffs. This is Moon Hole and higher up a series of original modern homes designed by the American architect Tom Johnston have been built. The diving off Mushroom Rock, Petit Nevis and the lee of Isle à Quatre is breathtaking. There is a day-time anchorage both at Petit Nevis and Isle à Quatre, weather permitting. Keep to the leeward clear sandy bottoms.

| 17 |
Mustique, Baliceaux and Battowia

The sail from Bequia to Mustique is usually upwind and a fairly rough ride, but well worth it. This is a glorious island, the home of the rich and famous. Remember to come in from the north to Brittania Bay in order to avoid the Montezuma Shoal. The best place to anchor is south of the jetty, as close to shore as possible with a stern line.

Once planted with cotton and sugar-cane, a magical cotton warehouse and its mills have been transformed into one of the world's finest luxury hotels, The Cotton House.

The Hazell family sold the island to the Hon. Colin Tennant in 1960. Colin Tennant called upon his friend, Oliver Messel, who at the time was chief designer at the Covent Garden Opera House in London. They decided that the properties to be built on the island

The islands of Battowia (top) and Baliceaux (bottom) from the air. (LESLEY SUTTY)

should remain strictly in line with the only remaining buildings of the original estate. During the 1960s and 1970s famous gingerbread and stone houses were built, and the Fort overlooking Britannia Bay was restored and a mansion built inside its walls. There is a rare and transparent quality in the atmosphere, from one deserted bay to the next. Landing at the jetty you will immediately come across Basil's Bar, which is an enchanting meeting place for yachtsmen and the island's inhabitants. It is possible to make a reservation by radio on VHF 68. Both restaurant and bar are worth a visit. Hanging over the reef, this bamboo structure provides wonderful views of the Grenadines, and excellent music. It is renowned for its parties and Basil is the best of hosts.

Walk up the hill to the left past the excellent but fairly expensive grocery store and souvenir shop, through a forest of flamboyant trees. As you bear left again down the hill you will come across the prettiest airport in our hemisphere. The landing strip is astonishing, and the Liat Twin Otters from St Vincent land here. Hang on to your seat if you do come in by air. The landing strip is short and downhill. The Twin's fame and prestige comes from its seeming ability to land on a postage stamp. A more exciting landing is to be had with Airlines of Cariacou and Region Air, who also run a BN2 service in and out of the island. A number of charter flights make the trip from Barbados and St Vincent. There is a small clinic near the airport and a resident doctor. The road carries on to the fabulous Cotton House Hotel. Here Colin Tennant, with tremendous flair and originality, made the ground floor of this handsome colonial building into a very original lounge and bar. Dining is on the surrounding terraces which overlook lily ponds, green lawns (in season!), white beaches and crystal clear lagoons.

In 1979 Colin Tennant sold this opulent property to the Martinican Guy de la Houssaye. He then moved to the north-west coast of the island, where he built a far more incredible structure, a Maharaja's palace in a palm grove with marble and coral blocks, in the purest tradition. Without knowing it he was building on one of the oldest prehistoric settlements in the Grenadines. The volcanic eruptions of 1979 created sea-level falls. A number of intact secondary funeral urns, some 1500 years old, were found buried in the sand as the tide retreated. They were recovered and sent to the British Museum. Colin Tennant, a man of considerable fantasy and charm, was eventually to settle on St Lucia with Bupa the

The wreck of the *Antilles* off Mustique (LESLEY SUTTY)

elephant and a wealth of wonderful furnishings brought from India, where his family had long been established and he had spent much of his youth.

Most of the villas on the island my be rented through the Mustique Company, which has an office close to the hotel. Each villa has its own cook, maid service, gardener, chauffeur and jeep.

Further on at Cheltenham Point is the wreck of the cruise ship *Antilles* which ran aground between the Piloris and the point in 1971. The *Queen Elizabeth II (QEII)* changed course and rescued all passengers within twenty-four hours. Recovery of the metal and scrap of the ship was envisaged by a number of magnates. The tale is that a wealthy Japanese industrialist bought the wreck for one dollar, but died in an aircrash before deciding how to go about dismantling the wreck, as stipulated in the Bill of Sale. The wreck still remains solidly anchored to the coral reef.

For a year or two the adventurous were able to climb on board and explore the vessel and dive in and out of the hold. Much as a new small island that had grown from the sea bed, the hull started to create strong tidal currents and break up, becoming increasingly dangerous to approach.

Baliceaux and Battowia

These two islands are only approachable during calm weather, when even then it is only possible to anchor off, leaving a watch on board, anchor your dinghy and swim ashore. There are heavy swells on the leeward shores, and although Baliceaux' lee anchorage has a good sandy beach, it shelves steeply. There is a small creek on Battowia in the south-eastern corner, with a chimney; this is where you can swim ashore. It can take as long as three to four hours to sail upwind to these islands from Bequia. From Mustique it is best to visit the area by motor launch.

| 18 |
Petit Mustique, Savane Island, Petit Canouan and Canouan

Petit Mustique and Savane

These islands are south of Mustique. Petit Mustique has strong currents to both north and south and is surrounded by coral reef. It is best to take a motor boat from Mustique to explore the beautiful coral gardens. Savane provides a good daytime anchorage off its west or leeward coast, in sand. The coral reefs are worth the visit. Access to the sandy beach is via the northern end of the reef.

Petit Canouan

This small islet is a bird sanctuary. On no account disturb the many nesting birds here.

The strong currents around this island attract the pelagic (open sea) fish, and you may be lucky trolling close to shore. This is a favourite haunt for barracudas and rainbow runners.

Canouan

Once past Petit Canouan you may encounter a flow of rip tides and choppy seas off Jupiter Point in the north. Once you are under the lee of the island remain vigilant as the 260 metres peaks of Mount Royal provoke wind rushes which have been known to break masts. The same applies to the south at Glossy Point, where the Sugar Loaf provokes a similar wind blast.

There is an excellent anchorage off the second sandy beach on the upper north of Charlestown Bay. Anchor in eight metres of sand. The holding is good, but take into account change of tide and allow for a 360° rotation on your anchor. The coral reefs along the shores here are very beautiful. Shallow draft vessels can go through the

Grand Bay, Canouan (CHRIS HUXLEY)

pass to the inner lagoon, leaving the black marker buoy to starboard. The calmest anchorage is in six metres just behind the reef on the left of this passage. The alignment is the old jetty and abandoned fish storage plant. Although the beaches on the northern coast are magnificent, this is a dangerous area to approach as it is directly open to the channel. It is possible in very calm weather to visit this virgin territory by small dinghy, and even then it may prove impossible to anchor as there is a residual ground swell all year round.

To explore the island, take the path leading from the jetty in the north and at the top of the hill turn left. A major Saudi-Japanese development is changing the face of this island. The 18th century church is now used for storage and the cemetery has been bulldozed. The only known prehistoric rock carving in the Grenadines has reportedly left the island. The beauty of this track, once incomparable as it curved its way round the foothills of Mount Royal is now the site of a golf course and condominiums. At Windward Bay there is a view of the Grenadine archipelago to north and south, a Japanese fish processing plant dominates the lagoons of the island's east coast. Windward Bay is the first of the sandy beaches, a fine picnic spot. In season there will be a number of

80

North Anchorage, Canouan (LESLEY SUTTY)

unusual species of butterflies, and numerous lizards sunning themselves.

As you enter the only village on the island you will see cultivated fields and pastures to the right. Turn left down the hill past the guest house Villa le Bijou. In the village there is a police station and one or two shops with essential provisions such as corned beef, rice, sugar and flour.

A new luxury hotel, the Tamarind Beach, recently opened at Charleston Bay. With this has come a telephone service to the island. Canouan Beach Hotel is situated on the southern peninsula, and accommodates its guests in bungalows. Owned by the Frenchman Gilles Sarazin since 1984, C.B.H. as it is called, had to overcome a number of teething problems before eventually settling down. Extremely isolated, which made this island so perfect, supplies were something of a headache. The hotel looks out over a fabulous beach towards the Tobago Cays. There is, however, an uncomfortable swell for those who choose to anchor offshore. The beach shelves down quickly and there is often a strong current coming in from the east. The hotel deals with this problem by taking its guests to the Tobago Cays, and using the beaches on the northern side of the peninsula, which offer excellent opportunities for marine

Windward Anchorage, Canouan (J AND Y BOURVEAU)

exploration. There is an airstrip on Canouan, with night landing facilities. A major development scheme is now targeting all the beautiful coasts of this rare Utopia.

Father Marc de Silva at the Roman Catholic church has a wealth of literature and information to offer visitors interested in the natural history and early Amerindian settlers.

| 19 |
Tobago Cays

The word cay, from the French *caille* is pronounced 'key' (as used to lock doors) and in fact the cays do in many cases serve to protect most anchorages on the windward shores, and in some areas landlock them.

The Tobago Cays are world famous, and this exceptional area of desert islands and coral reefs has now become a National Park. The marine environment has been severely affected over a period of twenty years, since the discovery of this area by yachts evolved into part of the schedule for cruise ship visitors. The Government is now promoting a programme for the control of the environment and eventual repopulation of the very diverse marine life. The islet of Jamesby was once home to a large colony of land iguanas. It would be interesting to try a breeding programme here. Yachts may anchor in two areas. The first is the passage between Petit Rameau and Petit Bateau in seven metres of sand. The holding is good, although only a few boats may anchor here at the same time as the tide is active and a stern line is necessary. The easier anchorage is inside the main lagoon south-west of Baradel and north-east of Jamesby in sand. There are strong tidal currents which come in over the shallower areas of the barrier reef, west and east; bathers should exercise caution. Diving off Horseshoe Reef is spectacular and trips are organised out of Union Island with certified monitors. World's End Reef offers a constantly changing scenery of coral gardens, sponges, delicate marine life and the impressive large fish species, sting rays, barracudas and sharks.

Diving outside this barrier reef is for confirmed divers, and should be accompanied by a manned security vessel.

Petit Tabac is a daytime anchorage for the initiated.

There are few records of shark aggression in the archipelago. However, remember that a southern stingray has a tail which bears a poisonous spine on its upper edge – an extraordinary serrated weapon, used by indigenous peoples as a means of defence for

Ashton Lagoon, looking towards Palm and Tobago Cays (overleaf) (LESLEY SUTTY)

centuries. If the stingray raises its tail this is a warning to keep off. The handsome spotted eagle ray may be seen here. They reach impressive sizes, and have what seems an unending whip tail. These marine animals are not dangerous and their prey is mainly molluscs. Stingrays have the habit of nesting in the sand with only their eyes visible. On one occasion, watching lemon sharks progress through a narrow passage, the current was strong and I had anchored myself to what I thought was hard rock. To my great surprise this shook me off, and a disgruntled snout belonging to a good-tempered southern stingray exploded from beneath me. By this time it was difficult to know where to look: ahead, behind, right or left? It is wounded fish that attract the sharks lying off these reefs, not men. Both sand sharks and rays are aesthetic and graceful in their own environment, and observing them, once you are accustomed to their presence, is most rewarding. The variety and colourings of the reef fishes, parrot, angel, baliste and wrasses is infinite. Be careful not to destroy their home, the coral reef. Mooring buoys are placed strategically in the sand for use by yachts. A major project for a marine reserve is evolving for the Tobago Cays. On no account put garbage on shore. There is a service dealing with this on Union Island.

| 20 |
Mayero (or Mayreau) and Catholic Island

Mayero (or Mayreau)

Once privately owned by the Eustace family, land reform by the present government provided the some 120 islanders with the possibility of investing in their smallholdings. Groundnuts are grown on the windward side of this tiny island. One village dominates the several bays and shores with fabulous views from the Roman Catholic church. This religion was inherited from the original French settlers, the St Heliers. Most of the men fish and trade between the islands. Coming in by sea there are two anchorages. The first anchorage is in the middle of Salt Whistle Bay. A coral reef juts out from the north of the bay. Anchor in the middle on thalassia or eel grass.

A Canadian company bought the land here in 1972. Ondina and Tom Potter started to build a secluded resort hidden in verdant gardens which took years of fortitude and love to establish on an island that was totally without resources. Ondina is probably the most efficient radio operator in the Grenadines. Salt Whistle Bay stands by on channels VHF 68 and 16. The telephone was installed on the island in September 1991.

Saline Bay is the main anchorage, but remember to clear the reef on the northern end of this bay at Grand Col Point. The best anchorage is west of the main jetty which leads to the village. Anchor off between the two jetties. The southern end of the bay is open to uncomfortable ground swells. Princess Cruises leased the pastures of this bay to install facilities for their ships. This area was a prehistoric settlement, and a number of roughly hewn hand axes were discovered here. The new installations have obscured the site. Access to the beach is via the village jetty; the southern jetty is private. It is often advisable to put out a stern anchor when tying up at the smaller jetties because of the swells and current. This is the case at Mayero. Leave the fenced area to your right and take the path to the left if you wish to visit the village. Denis' Hideaway

Saline Bay, Mayreau (CHRIS HUXLEY)

A charcoal pit, Mayreau (LESLEY SUTTY)

will provide refreshments when you arrive at the summit. The alternative hike is the path to the right which skirts the old salt pond and leads to sparkling lagoons and beaches which encompass the whole island. The diving in the coral gardens here is excellent. These are a little distance offshore, and it is best to be a group.

Catholic Island

Off the western shores of this island there is an explosion of marine life from a depth of nine metres. Forests of gorgonia soft and hard corals festoon the seabed inhabited by schools of shimmering fish. The current can be very strong here, and again a security vessel should be maintained on the surface.

The channel dividing Mayero from Union and the Tobago Cays is extremely unpredictable. Sea conditions can give a very uncomfortable ride if you decide to sail upwind to the Cays from the southern Monkey Point. The easier route is via the north of Mayero. Heading downwind to Union you will usually encounter surprisingly high swells in the channel due to the fact that the seabed is funnel shaped, plunging from 11 to 42 metres in the middle. Also the barrier reef has a break in it which allows the Atlantic briefly to take control; this provokes strong westerly currents. It is advisable to chart a route corresponding to the east of Palm Island if you observe a westerly drift. The east flowing current is not as strong.

| 21 |
Union Island

Approaching Union Island exercise caution and keep well to port of the three marker buoys which indicate the barrier reef and head for the Clifton Harbour jetty leaving the red blinking buoy to your port side (port = left, starboard = right!). It is best to come up round the western side of the central reef in this lagoon, and anchor close to Green Island which sits in the middle of the barrier reef. The approach from the eastern side of this inner reef is not recommended; yachts have often hit the northern edge and run aground. On no account try to enter this harbour after sunset. The number of yachts that have foundered on these reefs has caused general disinterest locally. The width of the reef, which makes this one of the best anchorages in the Grenadines, also makes it merciless as the Trade Winds will drive you further into trouble. Local rescue operations can be extremely costly, and in many cases it has been necessary to abandon the vessel.

Due to the expansion of the charter business and an airport, there is a heavy increase in traffic in a small port that was once given a wide berth.

Union Island has the most remarkable silhouette of the islands. Two thousand years ago it was designated as a religious centre by the Indians. Pre-ceramic tribes settled on Point Lookout. Most of the historic ruins are now buried under bush and shrubs. Fort Hill still has its original battery in place and the path to this peak leads to breathtaking views. There are two villages, Clifton and Ashton. The latter is the true capital. The seat of government for the Southern Grenadines is at Clifton, where both the District Officer and Senator live.

The administrative offices are at the end of the jetty, together with the post office. This is a point of entry. After hours it is possible to enter at the airport. Immigration officers are on duty here between 7 a.m. and 5 p.m. Transit passengers must stay within the airport if they do not wish to pay a stop over tax of EC $20. Union Island airport has caused much debate recently, as the government decided to redirect the airstrip and demolish Red Island in order to add additional footage, over the coral reef. The offshore island has now been levelled and the lagoon totally enclosed. The airport is government owned. Charlotte Honnart, who is French, has managed the Anchorage Yacht Club for seven years, and transformed what was a small private business into an efficient and delightful turning point for guests coming and leaving from every part of the world. There is a comprehensive yacht service: diesel, water, ice, fax, telephone and mail, with ATM STARDUST and Star Voyage charterboat offices. The bar and restaurant sit over an enclosure where sand sharks, turtles and mullet laze. There is a boutique with interesting handicrafts from throughout the Caribbean. There is a steel band on Friday nights, and piano music most other times. Reservations can be made on Channel 68. Liat and Air Martinique operate out of Union twice a day. In season Air Martinique has several connecting flights to Paris each week, with a short stopover in Martinique. You do not have to change airports.

Jaques Daudin provisioned yachtsmen at Park East until his retirement in May 1996 to edit his unique archives on the natural and social history of Union Island. A Frenchman, he provided, amongst other things, an excellent selection of French cheeses and tobacco. Born in China, Jaques is a famous, fervent naturalist and

An aerial view of Union Island (LESLEY SUTTY)

91

biologist who contributed to the evolution of the banana industry in the Windwards. He founded the first air company to link the Grenadines with Martinique, Satair, in 1972. A humanitarian, he has done much to help the island's children.

A short walk in blazing heat will take you into the centre of the village of Clifton. The Adams family run the Clifton Beach Hotel, Grand Union Supermarket, Hardware Store and Travel Agency. The father, Conrad Adams, Justice of the Peace and OBE, was a kind and generous man who with his wife Emeuthial pioneered the development of Clifton. Their daughters Stephanie, Leonie and Marie have continued in their steps. Stephanie is now Senator for the Southern Grenadines. Clifton has a number of shopping centres. Shell gas cylinders are available at the Grand Union, and gasoline at Mitchells Hardware Store and the Determination Bar. The stores face each other. There are no petrol pumps on Union; this is served from 100 litre drums. The Sunny Grenadines Bar and Restaurant, run by King Mitchell, sells ice.

The walk up the hill to Clifton Clinic is unforgettable. The islanders are great walkers and most of the roads on the island have astonishing gradients. There is a small, well-furbished fruit and vegetable market in Clifton. Fishermen supply conch, lobster and fresh fish. The recent intrusion and show of wealth from the

The Union Island basketball team (LESLEY SUTTY)

increasing number of tourists and yatchsmen coming to reprovision here has perturbed a number of the younger generation, suffering from unemployment. There are two sides to this recurring story which is not insoluble. Respect for the local population and their customs is essential. At the same time the majority of tourists coming to the Grenadines will not return, as this may be the trip they have saved up for most of their lives whilst they live and work in grey pitiless cities, travelling in subways, breathing in clouds of pollution. They deserve our good humour.

There is a rich community spirit in both villages. Ashton can be reached by minibus service. The ride is EC$2 per person. The drive between Clifton and Ashton goes along the shore with an unbroken view over the southern lagoon and Frigate Rock. Ashton is nestled into the slopes of the towering summit of Mount Parnassus.

Frigate Island and the Ashton Lagoon underwent a traumatic experience in 1994. A major development programme which planned to build condominiums on the pristine barrier reef, closed off the lagoon pass and started construction of docks for 300 yachts using part of Frigate Rock and the lagoon substrate as in-fill. The destruction of a rare and irreplaceable ecosystem on the central Grenada Bank drew international attention. Considerable damage had been done before the project was halted following a UNEP recommendation. This once-glorious environment is now in need of rehabilitation and projects for aqua culture have been proposed to help the villagers turn the situation round to their advantage.

The inside of the barrier reef is very beautiful. The current can be surprisingly strong. Do not try to swim across to Ashton. Most local sailors are cautious of the strong rip tides off the southern end of the barrier reef as you enter the channel for Carriacou and the Grenadines of Grenada.

There is a ferry service between Ashton and Hillsborough on Carriacou. Two small sloops trade between the capitals leaving on Monday and Thursday from Ashton jetty at 7.30 a.m., leaving Hillsborough at midday to return on the same day. For those wishing to stay over, customs and immigration formalities must be carried out at Clifton and Hillsborough as these towns are the capitals of different territories.

From Frigate Rock you can sail to Chatham Bay on the west coast in half an hour. Cross the mouth of the bay to avoid the middle coral reef (in two metres), and anchor at the north-eastern end of this mysterious bay. Chatham was once inhabited by Amerindians. Be careful not to interfere with seine nets, as this is a fogging ground for jack fish. There is a fringing reef that runs continuously along the beach, and you must land in the north-east corner opposite a dry salt pond. The high hills protecting this bay create strong winds as each cloud hits their summit. Sometimes these can rip off awnings. The bay is otherwise completely calm, tranquil and uninhabited, with varied and fascinating snorkelling. Don't be surprised when you leave the bay to find yourself motoring instead of sailing, and wondering where the wind has gone. This bay is not recommended in the summer if winds turn to the west.

Before leaving Union Island by air or sea be sure to visit a very engaging and elegant young lady who runs the handicraft boutique in the centre of Clifton, 'Chic Unique'. Margaret Wilson not only has a wide variety of batiks and summer wear, she also has a beautiful smile. But then this is the case of most Union islanders.

The Basin, Union Island (LESLEY SUTTY)

| 22 |
Palm Island

This is not paradise but fairyland and there is an intangible atmosphere on Palm Island which borders on legend. The sands are not white but silver with shades of pink and each flowering shrub and palm is inhabited by winged creatures. John Caldwell and his wife Mary, who lived a life of adventure at sea, discovered Prune Island in 1966. This was swampland and John leased the island from the government for 99 years. Mary was from Australia, John from Texas. With passion John set about planting coconuts everywhere he landed, and little by little there were coconut groves and shade where once we had baked in the sun. We rebaptised John Caldwell. He was to become 'Coconut Johnny' and his island Palm. Mary and John built simple, practical bungalows, with patios looking out over the sands and reefs. The service was elegant and the bar served the finest rum punches in the Caribbean. The middle swamp was filled and a short landing strip marked out. Mary had to crop her coconut

Aerial view of Palm and Union Islands (LESLEY SUTTY)

trees regularly so that the BN2s could land without the pilots doing the job for her. These nine-seater planes were the only access by air to the archipelago. Taking off with a Cessna or Baron was less than sure; flying was visual and a special licence was required to fly in and out. In 1975 when André Beaufrand and François Cheverry finished building their cement air-strip on Union Island, Mary and John sighed with relief as planes were re-routed. A ferry now collects the resort's passengers, and definitive peace reigns on Palm Island. Mary and John have two sons, Roger and Johnny Junior, who now help to run the island, which is self-sufficient in water and electricity. Reservations for dinner and barbecue can be made on VHF 68. It is also possible to take a day trip to the Tobago Cays with Roger and Donna on their well appointed yacht.

Ornithologists, bird-lovers – don't forget your cameras; humming birds, bananaquits, greckles, ground doves and mocking birds abound and have taken over here. Waders live in the swamp.

The best place to anchor is west of the jetty or south of it. North of this area the beach shelves immediately to 16 metres. Do not forget to look out for Grand Cay reef which breaks the surface between Union and Palm.

The hotel has an excellent boutique, grocery shop and diving facilities.

| 23 |
Petit Saint Vincent
(P.S.V.)

This is the most southern of the St Vincent Grenadines and a private resort for the wealthy. The island was bought from its owner on Petite Martinique in 1968 by an American company. The present owner Haze Richardson has run this unique and famous island for twenty years with rare originality, method and efficiency. He has constantly planned and improved the island for the comfort of his guests. A luxury power boat handles the passengers coming in by charter flight from Barbados or Martinique, transporting them from Union to P.S.V. in forty minutes, where guests are met by private jeep. *Wakiva* is captained faultlessly by Michael. The resort also has its own aircraft which is used for liaising between St Vincent and Union to ensure the smooth running of the island. Each individual bungalow has its special valet service. As in principle there are no telephones, in line with the total tranquillity you are looking for, this haven asks you to exert yourself as far as your private flagpole and mail box, hoist the former and put a list of your needs in the latter. The main office on the hill keeps a sharp lookout, and a blue and white jeep and manservant arrive promptly. This is what I call fun. Why ever leave? Tropical thatched shelters are strategically placed in hidden corners along the never-ending beaches, where you can lie in a hammock and dream as a limpid sea returns your reflection. If this is not enough you will be taken to total isolation which borders on unreality – a minute desert island with a single thatched roof, surrounded by endless coral gardens. Moon fish are waiting for you there.

Mopion Island (overleaf) (LESLEY SUTTY)

Useful information

St Vincent and the Grenadines Tourist Offices
(on Bay Street, Kingstown)
Address: P.O. Box 834, Kingstown, St Vincent and the Grenadines.
Tel: 457.1502   Fax: 456.2610

Ferry Boat Timetable

St Vincent ⇔ The Grenadines

	Depart		**Arrive**	
Friendship Rose (island schooner) and **Maxann O** (island schooner)				
MON–FRI	Bequia	6.30 am	St Vincent	7.45 am
	St Vincent	12.30 pm	Bequia	1.45 pm
MV Snapper (motor vessel)				
MON & THU	Bequia	6.00 am	St Vincent	7.00 am
	St Vincent	10.30 am	Bequia	11.30 am
	Bequia	11.45 am	Canouan	1.45 pm
	Canouan	2.00 pm	Mayreau	3.00 pm
	Mayreau	3.25 pm	Union Island	3.45 pm
TUE & FRI	Union Island	5.30 am	Mayreau	7.20 am
	Mayreau	7.30 am	Canouan	8.30 am
	Canouan	8.45 am	Bequia	10.45 am
	Bequia	11.00 am	St Vincent	12 noon
MV Admiral I (motor vessel)				
MON–FRI	Bequia	7.30 am	St Vincent	8.30 am
	St Vincent	9.00 am	Bequia	10.00 am
	Bequia	5.00 pm	St Vincent	6.00 pm
	St Vincent	7.00 pm	Bequia	8.00 pm
SATURDAY	Bequia	5.00 pm	St Vincent	6.00 pm
	St Vincent	7.00 pm	Bequia	8.00 pm
SUNDAY	Bequia	7.00 am	St Vincent	8.00 am
	St Vincent	9.00 am	Bequia	10.00 am
	Bequia	4.00 pm	St Vincent	5.00 pm
	St Vincent	5.15 pm	Bequia	6.15 pm

MV *Admiral II* (motor vessel)

MON–FRI	Bequia	6.30 am	St Vincent	7.30 am
	St Vincent	10.30 am	Bequia	11.30 am
	Bequia	2.00 pm	St Vincent	3.00 pm
	St Vincent	4.30 pm	Bequia	5.30 pm
SAT	Bequia	6.30 am	St Vincent	7.30 am
	St Vincent	12.30 pm	Bequia	1.30 pm

Boat fares

From	To	EC$
St Vincent	Bequia	10.00
(at night and weekends)		12.00
St Vincent	Canouan	13.00
St Vincent	Mayreau	15.00
St Vincent	Union Island	20.00

Note: Schedules are subject to change and cancellation without notice due to maintenance and other causes. Recheck times before travelling. Boats to Bequia and the Grenadines depart from the Grenadines dock in Kingstown harbour.

Sailing/yachting

Yachts are available for charter from:

St Vincent:

Yacht Charters	Tel: 456.9238/ 458.4989
Caribbean Sailing Yachts	Tel: 458.4308

Bequia:

Frangipani Yacht Services	Tel: 458.3244

Union Island:

Anchorage Yacht Club	Tel: 458.8221
A.T.M. Yachts	Fax: 458.8581
Stardust	Tel: 458.5881

Water sports

St Vincent:

Dive Beachcomber	Tel: 458.4283
Dive St Vincent	Tel: 457.4714
Mariners' Watersports	Tel: 458.4228

St Vincent Windsurfing School
Tel: 457.4688

Bequia:

Bequia Beach Club	Tel: 458.3248
Dive Bequia	Tel: 458.3504
Friendship Bay Hotel	Tel: 458.3222
Plantation House Hotel	Tel: 458.3425
Sunsports	Tel: 458.3255
Dive Paradise	Tel: 458.3563

Southern Grenadines:

Basil's Bar (Mustique)	Tel: 458.4621
Cotton House Hotel (Mustique)	Tel: 456.4777
Salt Whistle Bay (Mayreau)	VHF CH 68
Dive Anchorage (Union)	Tel: 458.8221
Palm Island Beach Club	Tel: 458.8824
Petit St Vincent Resort	Tel: 458.8801

Car/Jeep rental services

Companies include:

Avis   Tel: 456.9334/458.4945
David's Auto Clinic   Tel: 457.1116
Hertz   Tel: 456.1884
Johnson's U-Drive Rental
                 Tel: 458.4864
Kim's Rentals Ltd   Tel: 456.1884
Lucky Car Rental
            Tel: 457.1913/456.1215
Star Garage   Tel: 457.1169
Sunshine Jeep Rentals
                 Tel: 456.5380
UNICO Rentals   Tel: 456.5744

Scooter rentals

J.G. Agencies   Tel: 456.1409

Air services

Air Martinique:
St Vincent   Tel: 458.4528
Union Island   Tel: 458.8826
British Airways, Liat:
E.T. Joshua Airport   Tel: 458.4841
Reservations, K'town Tel: 457.1821
Union Island Airport Tel: 458.8230

Mustique Airways Tel: 458.4380

St Vincent Grenadines Air
                 Tel: 456.5610

Airlines of Carriacou
                 Tel: 444.2898

Travel agents and ground tour operators

St Vincent:
W. J. Abbott & Sons Ltd,
   Upper Bay Street, K'town
                 Tel: 456.1511
Barefoot Holidays,
   Blue Lagoon   Tel: 456.9334

Campbell's Travel,
   Egmont Street, K'town
                 Tel: 457.1067
Caribbean International Travel
   Services,
Granby Street   Tel: 457.1841
Corea & Co (1988) Ltd,
   Halifax Street, K'town
                 Tel: 456.1201
Emerald Travel & Tours,
   Halifax Street, K'town
                 Tel: 457.1996
Global Travel Service,
   White Chapel, K'town
            Tel: 456.1602/456.1622
Grenadine Travel Co Ltd,
   Arnos Vale   Tel: 458.4818
Hibiscus Tours,
   Kingstown   Tel: 456.4193
Kim's Rental Ltd,
   Grenville Street, K'town
                 Tel: 456.1884
St Vincent Travel service,
   Halifax Street, K'town
                 Tel: 456.1216
Travel World (St Vincent) Ltd,
   Bay Street, K'town
                 Tel: 456.2600
Bequia
Grenadine Travel Co Ltd,
   Port Elizabeth Tel: 458.3795
Union
Eagles Travel,
   Clifton   Tel: 458.8179

Taxis and minibuses

Rates are fixed by the government.
A full list of fares is available at
the Department of Tourism
Offices or from the Despatcher at
the airport.

Hotels, guest houses and apartments

St Vincent hotels

Address	Telephone	Facsimile
St Vincent & Grens. WI.	(809)	(809)

	Address	Telephone	Facsimile
Beachcombers Hotel,	PO Box 126.	458.4283	458.4385
Cobblestone Inn, Kingstown	PO Box 867.	456.1937	
Coconut Beach Inn, Indian Bay	PO Box 355.	457.4900	
The Lagoon Marina and Hotel	PO Box 133.	458.4308	456.9255
Emerald Valley Resort and Casino	Peniston Valley.	458.7421	
Grand View Beach Hotel, Villa Point	PO Box 173.	458.4811	457.4174
Haddon Hotel, Kingstown	PO Box 144.	456.1897	
Heron Hotel, Kingstown	PO Box 226.	457.1631	
Indian Bay Beach Hotel & Apts, Indian Bay Beach	PO Box 538.	458.4001	457.4777
Paradise Inn	PO Box 1286.	457.4795	457.4221
Petit Byahaut, Petit Byahaut Bay	Kingstown.	457.7008	457.7008
Rawacou, Stubbs	Stubbs.	458.4459	
Sunset Shores Hotel, Villa Beach	PO Box 849.	458.4411	457.4800
Villa Lodge Hotel, Villa Point	PO Box 222.	458.4641	457.4468
Young Island Resort, Young Island	PO Box 211.	458.4826	457.4567

St Vincent apartments

Address	Telephone	Facsimile
St Vincent & Grens. WI.	(809)	(809)

	Address	Telephone	Facsimile
The Botanic Apts, New Montrose	PO Box 359	457.9781	457.0812

103

St Vincent apartments

	Address	Telephone	Facsimile
Bambi's Beach Apts, Indian Bay	PO Box 111.	458.4934	
Belleville Apts, Villa	PO Box 262.	458.4776	
Breezeville Apts, Villa Point	PO Box 222.	458.4004	
Indian Bay Beach Hotel & Apts, Indian Bay Beach	PO Box 538.	458.4001	457.4777
Macedonia Rock Hotel, Cane Hall	Cane Hall.	458.4076	
Ratho Mill Apt, Ratho Mill	Ratho Mill.	458.4849	
Ricks Apts, Cane Hall	PO Box 63.	456.1242	456.2593
Ridge View Terrace Apts, Ratho Mill	PO Box 176.	456.1615/458.4212	
Tranquillity Apts, Indian Bay Beach	PO Box 71.	458.4021	
Tropic Breeze	PO Box 217.	458.4618	456.4592
Umbrella Beach Apts, Villa	Villa.	458.4651	

St Vincent guest houses

	Address	Telephone	Facsimile
	St Vincent & Grens. WI.	(809)	(809)
Bella Vista Inn	Kingstown Park.	457.2757	
Foot Steps	Georgetown.	458.6433	
Highfield Guest House	Lowmans Hill.	457.7563	
Kingstown Park Guest House	PO Box 41.	456.1532	
Sea Breeze Guest House	Arnos Vale.	458.4969	
The Moon	Arnos Vale.	458.4656	

The Grenadines
Hotels, villas, apartments and guest houses

	Address	Telephone	Facsimile
Bequia	St Vincent & Grens. WI.	(809)	(809)
Bequia Beach Club, Friendship	Bequia.	458.3248	458.3689

The Grenadines
Hotels, villas, apartments and guest houses

Bequia	Address	Telephone	Facsimile
Blue Tropic Apartments, Friendship	Bequia.	458.3248	458.3689
Crescent Beach Inn, Crescent Bay	Bequia.	458.3400	
De Reef Apartments, Lower Bay	Bequia.	458.3447/458.3484	
Frangipani, Port Elizabeth	Bequia.	458.3255	458.3824
Friendship Bay Hotel, Friendship	Bequia.	458.3222	458.3840
Julie's Guest House, Port Elizabeth	Bequia.	458.3304	
Gingerbread Apartments	Bequia.	458.3800	458.3775
Keegan's Guest House, Lower Bay	Bequia.	458.3254	
Kingsville Apartments, Lower Bay	Bequia.	458.3404	
Lower Bay Guest House, Lower Bay	Bequia.	458.3675	
Old Fort, Mount Pleasant	Bequia.	458.3440	458.3824
Plantation House Hotel, Belmont	Bequia.	458.3425	458.3612
Spring on Bequia, Spring	Bequia.	458.3414	

Southern Grenadines	Address	Telephone	Facsimile
	St Vincent & Grens. WI.	(809)	(809)
Anchorage Yacht Club, Clifton	Union Island.	458.8221	458.8804
Clifton Beach Hotel, Clifton	Union Island.	458.8235 456.1833	458.8365
The Cays Apts	Union Island.	456.2221	457.4266
Lambi's Guest House	Union Island.	458.8549	
Snagg's Guest House	Union Island.	458.8255	
Sunny Grenadines, Clifton	Union Island.	458.8327	458.8398
Cotton House	Mustique.	456.4777	456.4777
Firefly House	Mustique.	458.4621	
Mustique Company (Villa Rentals)	Mustique.	458.4621	456.4565
Anchor Inn	Canouan.	458.8568	
Canouan Beach Hotel	Canouan.	458.8888	458.8875

	Address St Vincent & Grens. WI.	Telephone (809)	Facsimile (809)
Southern Grenadines			
Crystal Sands	Canouan.	458.8015	458.8309
Tamarind Beach Hotel	Canouan.	458.8044	458.8851
Villa La Bijou	Canouan.	458.8025	
Palm Island Beach Club	Palm Island.	458.8824	458.8804
Petit St Vincent Resort	Petit St Vincent.	458.8801	458.8801
Salt Whistle Bay, Mayreau	Mayreau.	VHF Ch 68	

Restaurants

St Vincent

Basil's Bar & Restaurant	Villa	Juanita's	Grenville Street
Basil's Too	Bay Street	Juliette's	Middle Street
Bonadie's Restaurant	Bedford Street	Kenmars	Halifax Street
Bounty	Halifax Street	Kentucky Fried Chicken	Grenville Street
Cobblestone Roof Bar	Bay Street	Lime 'N' Pub	Villa Beach
Chicken Roost	Grenville Street and Arnos Vale	Manna Quick Snack	Halifax Street
		Molly's Restaurant	Bay Street
CSY Beach Bar	Blue Lagoon	Nice Foods Unlimited	Middle Street
CSY Restaurant	Blue Lagoon		
Dano's Restaurant	Middle Street	Pizza Party	Arnos Vale
Emerald Valley Resort and Casino	Peniston	Reigate	Halifax Street
		Restaurant a la Mer	Indian Bay Beach
		Rio Foods	Higginson Street
Foot Steps	Georgetown	Sunset Shores	Villa
French Restaurant	Villa Beach	Vee Jays	Bay Street
Frenz	Frenches Gate	Villa Lodge	Villa Point
Global Cafe	Paul's Avenue	Wave	Blue Lagoon
Heron Hotel	Bay Street	Young Island Resort	Young Island
J Bee's Restaurant	Grenville Street		

Bequia

Bequia Beach Club
Café King Fisher
Coco's Place
Cool Spot Restaurant and Bar
Crescent Beach Inn
Daphne's
Dawn's Creole Bar and Restaurant
De Reef
Flame Tree Restaurant
Frangipani Hotel Restaurant
Friendship Bay Restaurant
Gingerbread Restaurant and Bar
The Green Boley
Green Flash

The Harpoon Salon
Industry Beach Bar
Julie's
Keegan's
Le Petit Jardin
Mac's Pizzeria and Bake Shop
Old Fig Tree
Old Fort Restaurant
Plantation House Restaurant
The Port Hole
Schooner's
Spring
Theresa's
The Whaleboner

Union Island

Anchorage Yacht Club
Boll Head Bar
Clifton Beach Restaurant
Eagles Nest Entertainment Centre

Lambi's Restaurant
Sunny Grenadines Hotel
  Restaurant
T&N

Mustique

Basil's Bar & Restaurant
Cotton House

Canouan

Canouan Beach Hotel
Palapa Restaurant
Villa Le Bijou

Mayreau

Dennis' Hideaway
J&C Bar and Restaurant
Island Paradise Restaurant and Bar

Health Clubs

Grand View Club, Villa Point   Tel: 458.4811
Prospect Racquet Club, Calliaqua Bay Tel: 458.4866

Banking

Currency

The East Caribbean Dollar (EC$) is the currency used locally. It is linked to the US$. At the Banks you will get EC$2.67 for US$1.00 cash and EC$2.68 for US$1.00 travellers cheques. You are advised to exchange your currency at the banks.

Credit cards

Major credit cards are generally accepted by most hotels and some car rental companies.

American Express

The local representative is Caribbean International Travel Services on Granby Street, Kingstown.

Bank hours

Monday to Friday 8am–12.00/1.00 pm
Friday 2.00 pm/3.00 pm to 5 pm
At E.T. Joshua Airport
Monday–Saturday 7.00 am–5.00 pm
Extended hours–Christmas,
Easter and Carnival.

Banks

Bank of Nova Scotia
  Halifax Street, Kingstown
        Tel: 457.1601
Barclays Bank plc
  Halifax Street, Kingstown
        Tel: 456.1706
Branch: Bequia   Tel: 458.3215
Canadian Imperial Bank of
  Commerce
  Halifax Street, Kingstown
        Tel: 457.1587

Caribbean Banking Corporation
  Ltd. South River Rd.,
  Kingstown
        Tel: 456.1501
First St Vincent Bank
  Granby Street, Kingstown
        Tel: 456.1873
National Commercial
  Bank of St Vincent
  Halifax Street, Kingstown
        Tel: 457.1844
Branches: Union Island,
  Bequia and E.T. Joshua Airport
Owens Bank Ltd
  Bay Street, Kingstown
        Tel: 457.1230
St Vincent Co-operative Bank
  Middle Street, Kingstown
        Tel: 456.1894

Postal information and hours

The General Post Office, on
Halifax Street in Kingstown is open
Monday to Friday 8.30 am–3.00 pm.
Saturday 8.30 am–11.30 am.
There are sub-post offices in all
towns and villages.

Government offices hours

Monday to Friday
8.00 am–12.00 and 1.00 pm–4.15 pm

Govt Treasury Dept hours

Monday to Friday 9.00 am–3.00 pm
Saturday 9.00 am–12.00

Inland Revenue and Licensing office hours

Monday to Friday 9.00 am–3.00 pm

Registry hours

Monday to Friday 9.00 am–12.00
  1.30 pm–4.00 pm
Saturday 9.00 am–11.00 am